Clem Harrison had a week's leave to look forward to, after the experience of the Royal Air Force Swinderby recruitment training, and he was determined to enjoy the next seven days, before embarking on another new life changing experience, at Royal Air Force Hereford, for trade training.

If Clem had to be honest with himself, he could not wait to travel to RAF Hereford, and he worked out the journey by phoning the British Rail ticket office, and found the connections he needed to take, to arrive at Hereford railway station efficiently. He discovered he had to take four trains. The first train was from Hull Paragon station to Stalybridge, then he needed to change there and take another train to Stockport, and change there, before taking a third train to Crewe, before changing there, and travelling to Hereford railway station, and taking a bus to Credenhill, where RAF Hereford was located. It was exciting for Clem to plan, and he could not wait to travel and get started with the training.

Clem spent the full week at home, but was mentally preparing himself for the rigours of another round of training again soon. But he was not too concerned about it, as if RAF Hereford was anything like RAF Swinderby, it was going to be another enjoyable, but tough experience, and it crossed his mind whether the drill was as strict at RAF Hereford, as it was at RAF Swinderby, and he wondered what the instructors were going to be like, and whether he could pass the exams. But he did not let the doubts and worries saturate his brain, he just considered he had too much time on his hands, and needed to occupy his mind to stop the fear of failure.

Clem decided to stop thinking and start doing, as he had done well at RAF Swinderby, and he was determined to carry on where he left off, and continue with being successful at every task, whatever was thrown at him at RAF Hereford, because he was determined to succeed.

But Clem had nowhere to go, as everybody was at work, so he decided to listen to music and prepare some writing for his new book, as he loved to write, and he continued with the story he had begun before joining the Royal Air Force, about a forest that was condemned by everyone except one man, and Clem settled himself down at his writing desk and beavered away, taking his mind off the thoughts of RAF Hereford, and the doubts that were coming to the forefront of his mind. Writing got all the tension out of his body and released the pressure of modern life. When Clem wrote, he wrote from his heart and soul, and it cleared away the waste that he did not need. It removed every toxic poison that had built up within him, and provided freedom to enjoy life. Without his writing, Clem would not know what to do with himself, as it was his salvation, when life suddenly got hard. It passed the time, and put the world to rights. The story about the haunted forest was taking off well.

When Clem got down to his writing, he managed to flow quickly, and the words came with ease. It was a natural thing for him to do, and even if these stories did not get published, the enjoyment he got out of being creative meant more than anything to him, than all the tea in China.

As it was mid November, the weather was turning chilly, and Clem began to pack his blue Royal Air Force rucksack, ready for the journey to RAF Hereford. The countdown was on. He packed warm clothes, sturdy shoes, thick jeans, for the leisure time in the evening and weekends, as he knew he would be staying there until his next leave, which would be at Christmas. So he had six weeks to spend at the RAF Hereford training camp, until coming home again. But that is why Clem joined up in the first place. To get a job, learn a trade, earn some money, and make something out of his life, successfully.

Clem was happy with today's writing, and was happy about the forthcoming trip to RAF Hereford. Four trains and three changes of train did not faze him whatsoever, he was up for it.

"Bring it on!" he declared.

Clem's bag was packed with neatly ironed shirts, with the uniforms placed at the very top, as he was prepared to travel in his civilian clothes. There had been no memo to issue an order to travel in his Number One uniform, so he pressed it, and packed it carefully.

With the train ticket bought, a few days later, when Clem travelled to the Hull city centre railway station at 9 am, his bag packed and his packing up and flask prepared, Clem was ready to go. It was Monday and the train was due to leave at 10.04 am. Clem boarded the train, found a seat and settled in it without any problems. He enjoyed travelling and was a patient sort, and this journey was going to test his patience to the limit, but he was ready. He made sure he packed his writing material, and he got down to some work on his story, about the condemned forest.

The train journey was going well for Clem. It was packed, as usual, and not a seat could be found. There were even some people standing. It meant only one thing, British Rail were making some money out of this journey.

Clem had settled down to do some writing, and was pleased he had brought his storybook material, as it helped to pass the time. He hardly ever suffered from writer's block, and he was appreciative about that, as this story was beginning to develop really well. It wasn't a scary story, just science fiction, and with that genre, anything could be written, as it was the nature of the beast, and nothing was impossible, when it came to science fiction. Clem filled his boots and made it as ridiculously far fetched as possible. The greater the better. It was fun to write science fiction, thought Clem.

The Hull to Stalybridge train took two hours, and Clem disembarked from the train to make his next connection, which was in thirty minutes. There was no rush. Half an hour was ample time for Clem to walk the platforms. It was just finding the correct platform, that was the snag. But he used his initiative, and checked the passenger information facility to find the train time, and platform number, before making his way in the right direction. He needed platform 2.

The train from Stalybridge to Stockport was on time, and Clem reckoned that was good service from British Rail. He had no complaints so far. When he boarded the train, it was a shuttle service, and did not have the comfortable seats of a long haul train. It was merely used for short haul journeys, as this one, was only half an hour.

The train arrived at Stockport railway station 27 minutes later, and yet again, it was on time. Clem had ten minutes to make the next connection, and he got his skates on to make it, before it departed, as the day was going well and he did not want to spoil it by missing his connection.

He raced down the platform, checked with the timetable for the platform number, and train time, and legged it to platform 1, as advised. The train from Stockport to Crewe again was on time.

The journey from Stockport to Crewe took 90 minutes, and Clem realised he was almost at his final destination. Only one more train to catch, the Crewe to Hereford train, and then a bus from Hereford to Credenhill, where RAF Hereford was based.

Clem had been travelling for four hours and was feeling peckish, so he tucked into his packing up and poured a cup of lukewarm tea from his flask. It was 3pm and if things stayed like they were, with all the connections meeting amicably, Clem reckoned he would be in Hereford bus station before 5.15pm.

The journey from Crewe to Hereford took 2 hours, and Clem's calculations were spot on. He had been six hours on the four trains with nearly an hour of hanging around the platforms, but none of it bothered Clem. He was lapping it up, and he had enjoyed every single second. It was new. It was novel. It was different.

At 5.30pm, Clem boarded a bus with the name Credenhill brightly written in neon on its front panel, and he paid his fare, sat back and waited for the fifth and final leg of his long journey, to be completed within 30 minutes.

Clem reported to the Guardroom, as the order stipulated in the "Welcome Pack" he had received in the post, a few days ago. He needed to register his attendance, and be designated a billet block to reside in, where he would spend the next six weeks, up until the Christmas break.

He signed in and received a "Visitor Pass" as a temporary measure, and was escorted by a Senior Aircraftman to the assigned billet block, and he immediately realised there was a slight relaxation in the discipline, compared to that of RAF Swinderby. He had expected to have been marched there with his shoulders back, and head up, like he was in the Coldstream Guards, but this was not the case, and the SAC on duty casually strolled alongside Clem, on the way to his new abode.

Clem had to admit to himself that he was suddenly feeling a little groggy, after all that travelling he had done, and he could not wait to sling his shoes under his bed, and stretch out on top of his cosy, warm mattress, with the fresh smell of sheets and a pillow case. He did not ask for much.

Clem breezed into the billet room for the first time, as if he had been there all of his life. He was feeling confident, brash and upbeat, and knew this was going to be a successful posting. He could not wait to get down to the training, and learn his new trade, supply.

The Senior Aircraftman showed Clem to his place, which was halfway down the large billet room. There were twelve beds in the room and some were occupied, with half a dozen or so nervous but excited airmen, awaiting for the dawn of their new Royal Air Force careers to begin. Clem thanked the SAC for his help, and quickly made himself at home, unpacking his RAF uniform, and civilian clothing. After a hot shower and a shave, Clem felt human again. He dressed in a blue jumper, white tee shirt and black jeans, and sprawled out across his single bed, contemplating the things to come in the next 24 hours. He relished the challenge, embraced the opportunity, and thanked his lucky stars for being where he was, at that present moment in time.

"Hey, hello mate. How are you doing?" asked the airman in the next bed to Clem, speaking with a broad south western English accent.

"I'm fine thanks, how are you?" replied Clem, in an equally friendly tone of voice.

"I'm great thank you. Have you had far to come?" asked Clem's new neighbour, a blonde tousled haired thin set youth, of about seventeen.

"Far enough, to be honest. I've travelled from Hull, in East Yorkshire," replied Clem.

"That is a very long way to travel. I'm from Swindon, which isn't too far from here, roughly about seventy odd miles, and my name is Stuart. Stuart Saunders," came the airmen's answer.

"Yes, it took me most of the day to get here. I set off from Hull at ten o'clock this morning, and arrived here just a few minutes ago. My name's Clem Harrison, by the way."

"That's some serious mileage there mate, and it's good to meet you Clem. Do you support Hull City?" asked Stuart.

"No, not really. I support Tottenham Hotspur, and Aston Villa," replied Clem.

"Do you? I support my home town team, Swindon Town," revealed Stuart, laughing out loud.

"Good for you! Hull City aren't doing too bad, but I've followed Tottenham Hotspur since I was about seven or eight years old, and Aston Villa for just over a year," explained Clem.

"Swindon Town have had their moments, namely the League Cup final, in 1969, when they famously beat Arsenal 3-1," stated Stuart, happily.

"Wow, Swindon beat Arsenal?" replied Clem.

"Yes, and Swindon were in Division Three at that time too, while Arsenal were in Division One," stated Stuart.

"That is one incredible result! Well done Swindon Town!" exclaimed Clem.

"Don Rogers was the star for Swindon, with two great goals," revealed Stuart.

"That name rings a bell," replied Clem.

"Yes, he's the best player Swindon Town have ever had. And the funny thing is, as the Football League Cup winners, we were supposed to be given a place in the

European Fairs Cup, but as we were only in the Third Division, the Football League wouldn't allow it, as only First Division Clubs could qualify," stated Stuart.

"That's unlucky!" replied Clem.

"It didn't take away our cup winning glory, though!" exclaimed Stuart.

"That's true. But what happened to Don Rogers?" asked Clem.

"He signed for Crystal Palace, a couple of years after the League Cup final win, and became a legend there, scoring the goal of the season in 1973. He then went on to join Queens Park Rangers, two or three years later, before re-joining Swindon Town, earlier this year," explained Stuart.

"So, Don Rogers is back at Swindon Town, *where it all began*?" asked Clem.

"Yep, he sure is," replied Stuart.

"Good for him, and for Swindon Town!" exclaimed Clem.

"But I think Crystal Palace got the best two seasons out of him, from 1972 to 1974. Although he did win us the League Cup final in 1969, I suppose, with two extra time goals, so it's not all bad," stated Stuart.

"And if Swindon Town had been in the First Division, who knows, they may have gone on to win the European Fairs Cup, in 1970!" suggested Clem.

"Yes, that's true!" replied Stuart.

"It's a funny old game!" said Clem.

"It sure is," agreed Stuart.

Clem had an early night, and was tucked up in his bed before 9pm, after taking a stroll to the NAAFI, for a can of Coca Cola, and a packet of crisps. He also bought a one pint carton of milk to take back to the billet with him, whilst he was there. He did not know anyone in the NAAFI, as everybody seemed to be in the same boat as Clem, and had just arrived, and were looking lost, so Clem returned to the billet block half an hour later, and turned in early for the night.

There was still noise and chattering between the new intake of trade trainees in the background, as they were getting to know each other, but it did not bother Clem, too much. He merely covered himself up with the bed covers, sunk his head into his fairly hard pillow, and dropped off to sleep, almost instantly.

There was no reveille to wake up Clem, the next morning. That had all finished when he had "passed out" from RAF Swinderby. Instead, Clem was left to fend for himself, when it came to waking up, and he was thankful for his inbuilt clock. After six weeks of intensive training at RAF Swinderby, Clem's body had trained itself to know when 6.15 am had arrived, and he checked his watch to find out that it was *exactly that time*. He had no idea on where he was going, what time he was starting the training, or more importantly, where the Airmen's Mess was situated, but he didn't worry about it, as he would find out all that, sooner or later.

He thought it would be a good idea to get up, have a wash and shave, and make tracks to find the Airmen's Mess, for a spot of breakfast. He was famished. Then he would be ready to find the answers to the other questions, in due course.

After dressing, and looking around for someone to accompany him to the Airmen's Mess, it appeared that only Stuart Saunders was ready.

"Are you having breakfast today?" asked Clem, in the direction of Stuart.

"Yep, are you?" replied Stuart.

"Yes, I sure am, I'm starving!" answered Clem.

"Come on then, let's go!" exclaimed Stuart.

The two airmen made their way quickly outside, into the freezing cold late November morning. There was ice in the air, a slight mist, and it was pitch black.

"Any idea where we are going?" asked Clem, scratching his head.

"I haven't got the foggiest to be honest, but when I can't find something, I usually ask for help," replied Stuart.

"Good idea," agreed Clem.

"Hey up, I'll ask these two," stated Stuart.

"Okay," replied Clem.

Stuart approached two airmen dressed in Royal Air Force uniform, that were walking towards him, and he stopped them politely.

"Excuse me, but do you know the way to the Airmen's Mess?" asked Stuart.

"No, sorry mate. We are new to these parts, and are looking for it ourselves," replied one of the airmen.

"Okay. Have you just been recently posted too?" asked Stuart.

"Yes mate," replied the airman.

"Same here, and we haven't got a clue where we are going," said Stuart.

"Snap! We both arrived here last night, and this is the start of our first full day," replied the same airman.

"Okay, well good luck!" stated Stuart, making his way in a different direction.

"And the same to you, too!" replied the airman.

"I hope you find the Airman's Mess!" stated Stuart.

"That's easier said, than done!" joked the same airman.

Clem and Stuart wandered one way, and the other two airmen headed in the opposite direction, towards the billets.

"If those airmen came from that direction, and didn't find the Airmen's Mess, don't you think it's a waste of time *going this way*?" asked Clem.

"It might be, but it all depends if those guys were telling the truth! They may have been pulling our legs. We are freshers, like fish out of water, and stand out a mile, with our new berets, shiny shoes, pressed trousers, and new jumpers, *but did you see those guys uniforms*?" asked Stuart.

"Nope, I didn't," replied Clem.

"They were as worn as I don't know what, and I think they were taking the Mickey out of us!" answered Stuart.

"Oh look, the Airmen's Mess!" said Clem, in bewilderment.

"See what I mean!?" exclaimed Stuart.

"Yep, I get what you're saying," agreed Clem.

"They were pulling a fast one, and would have had us wandering around the whole base, if they had had their way," replied Stuart.

"You're right!" stated Clem.

"But they didn't fool me. They stood out a mile too, by the state of their scruffy uniform. If they had been at RAF Swinderby looking like that, they would have been back-flighted two weeks!" exclaimed Stuart.

"Good point," agreed Clem.

"Come on, let's get some scran!" exclaimed Stuart.

The two airmen that were fledglings to RAF Hereford headed towards the Airmen's Mess, and they could not wait to sample the culinary delights of their new training base, and compare the food to that of RAF Swinderby.

It was fairly empty inside, with plenty of places to sit. The building was far larger than the Airmen's Mess at RAF Swinderby, but would it pass the crucial "Taste Test?" That was the burning question, and it was for Clem and Stuart to find out, and they could not wait to tuck into the food on offer.

The food did not disappoint Clem. It was tasty, rich and full of goodness, and Clem had to admit that it was better than the RAF Swinderby grub, and was almost as nice as his mother's cooking. Clem munched every last crumb and could easily have licked his plate clean. It was not very often he had thought to do that after a meal.

"That wasn't bad," said Stuart, as he pushed his plate away and grabbed the dish holding his cereal.

"I thought it was very good," replied Clem.

"What did you have?" asked Stuart.

"Sausages, bacon, eggs and tomatoes," replied Clem. "What about you?"

"Eggs and beans on toast, with brown sauce," replied Stuart.

"Nice! I must say though, it was one of the best meals I've ever tasted. Compliments to the chef!" exclaimed Clem.

"I wouldn't go as far as that, mate," replied Stuart jovially.

"It was exquisite!" reiterated Clem keenly.

Clem tucked into his cereal, which consisted of shredded wheat, with oodles of hot milk and sugar running over the top. He was a big fan of hot milk and sugar, and the more the merrier as far as he was concerned, when it came to that particular delicacy. Clem could not get enough of it, as he had a sweet tooth, and hot milk and sugar just encouraged him more to indulge in the stuff.

"That was fabulous!" enthused Clem, as he finished his cereal.

"What did you have, as it wasn't there long enough for me to look?" asked Stuart.

"Shredded wheat, with hot milk and sugar," replied Clem. "What about you?"

"Weetabix, with fresh cream," replied Stuart.

"That sounds nearly as good as mine! Was it nice?" asked Clem.

"Yes, it wasn't bad at all," replied Stuart, nodding in approval.

"Very good!" exclaimed Clem, getting up from his chair.

"Where are you going?" asked Stuart.

"For seconds. I enjoyed the breakfast so much, I fancy some more!" enthused Clem, as keen as mustard.

Clem returned with another plateful of sausages, eggs and bacon, but without the tomatoes, as they had all gone. He tucked enthusiastically into his second helping, with just as much gusto as the first helping.

Stuart poured himself a cup of tea from a large tea pot, and Clem watched him as he took his first sip.

"What's the tea like?" asked Clem, as he munched on a slice of bacon.

"It's good!" replied Stuart.

"Any sign of the dreaded bromide?" asked Clem.

"No, strangely enough," replied Stuart.

"That makes a change from RAF Swinderby!" exclaimed Clem.

"It sure does, although you did kind of get used to it, after a while," replied Stuart, with a smirk.

"That's very true, and we'll have to get used to another taste now," joked Clem.

"But that won't be any hardship, I'm sure!" exclaimed Stuart.

Clem laughed, nodded his head in agreement and finished tucking into his second helping of breakfast, before pouring himself a cup of tea from the same pot as Stuart.

"Yep, you're right, there's definitely no sign of any bromide in this tea!" stated Clem confidently, and nodding his head in approval, as he took his first taste.

Stuart laughed because he knew what it meant to taste bromide in the tea, and it had not been a pleasant experience at RAF Swinderby, with the tea served there. This would be a refreshing change.

"I can't understand why there isn't bromide in the tea here. It's still an RAF station," said Clem.

"But there are WRAFs stationed here, and they won't want to taste bromide when they're pouring out their daily cuppa, will they?" replied Stuart.

"*Are there WRAFs here?*" asked Clem in surprise.

"Yep, there sure is!" replied Stuart.

"Well, I didn't know that! You learn something new everyday, don't you?" stated Clem.

"You sure do. I was surrounded by a load of them as I travelled on the bus here yesterday afternoon, and when they got off at my stop outside the RAF station gates, I knew I was going to be in for a noisy time in the Guardroom! Those girls can half make some din!" exclaimed Stuart.

"Can they?" replied Clem.

"Yes! *Have you got any sisters*?" asked Stuart.

"Nope," replied Clem.

"I've got two sisters, and they do half go on sometimes, and make more noise than a team of rugby players!" remarked Stuart.

"You're kidding me!" replied Clem.

"I'm not, it's true! The palaver, the noise and the drama. It's like living in a soap opera, with those two sisters of mine!" exclaimed Stuart.

"Really? It must *just be your sisters*," joked Clem.

"Maybe so, but you'll find out for yourself with the WRAFs here, just how melodramatic females can be," stated Stuart.

"I can't wait to find out. It should be fun discovering the wonderful world of women, and getting to know about all their traits and characteristics!" enthused Clem.

"Believe me, you'll need to have the patience of a saint, if my two sisters are anything to go by," stated Stuart.

"Let me decide that for myself!" replied Clem.

Clem finished his second helping of breakfast, and had to admit to himself that he was full. He had thoroughly enjoyed his first meal at RAF Hereford, and he was very impressed with the quality of the food on offer.

"Are you ready to go back to the billet?" asked Clem towards Stuart.

"Yep, I was ready ten minutes ago, before you indulged in your second helping of the fry up," replied Stuart.

"Oh, sorry, but I just couldn't resist it, as I was famished after yesterday's long journey, when I had next to nothing to eat, and had only managed a couple of curled up sandwiches, and a cup of lukewarm tea from my flask. So I really needed this extra helping of brekkie!" replied Clem.

"No worries, it's okay!" stated Stuart, getting up from his chair.

"Let's get back to the billet, and see if anyone knows what's happening with regards to the trade training, as I've not got the foggiest," suggested Clem.

"What trade are you?" asked Stuart.

"Supply," replied Clem. "What about you?"

"Steward," stated Stuart.

"Stuart the steward! Is that like a waiter?" asked Clem, laughing.

"Yes, a glorified waiter, to be honest!" replied Stuart.

"Do you know what's happening, *with your training*?" asked Clem.

"Nope, I've not got a clue where I'm supposed to be, or what time I'm supposed to start," replied Stuart.

"Well, I'm sure we'll find out, in due course," said Clem.

"Yes, I reckon there'll be someone sent to collect us, and take us all off in different directions, to some classroom or other, to begin the training," replied Stuart.

"Or otherwise a note might be pinned on the notice board, back at the billet, telling us where to report to," said Clem.

"If we've got a notice board, that is," replied Stuart.

"Yes, I'm sure we have," stated Clem.

"Come on then, let's go and find out!" replied Stuart.

The two airmen returned to the billet block, and immediately looked for a notice board in the entrance hall, and although there was one, as Clem had mentioned earlier, unfortunately for them, there was nothing posted on it.

"What do we do now, that's Plan A gone for a Burton?" exclaimed Stuart.

"We do as you advised earlier, when we couldn't find the Airmen's Mess! We ask somebody!" replied Clem firmly.

"Oh yes, I forgot about that. It must be because I'm all of a fluster, and a panic," said Stuart with honesty.

"Stop worrying mate. The powers that be will have everything under control. This is trade training, not basic training. We are at RAF Hereford now, not RAF Swinderby!" emphasised Clem philosophically.

"Yes, that's true. Thanks for the advice," replied Stuart.

"Let's ask around. It worked before with those two airmen, even though they lied through their back teeth," suggested Clem.

"Come on then, let's get this sorted out, once and for all," replied Stuart.

Clem led the way this time, and Stuart followed. There were not many people about in the billet, only one or two, as the others were at the Airmen's Mess, but neither of the airmen that they were approaching appeared frantic about the day's arrangements, for the trade training.

"Hey guys, how are you doing?" called Clem.

"Not bad, what about you?" replied a white skinned, Afro haired, tall airman, of over six feet in height.

"That's good, and I'm fine thanks. I'd just like to introduce myself, my name's Clem," he revealed.

"Pleased to meet you, Clem, I'm Callum," was the reply from the Afro haired airman.

"And I'm Calvin," piped up the second airman, that was the spitting image of Callum.

"Wow, are you two twins?" asked Clem.

"Yep, identical twins! How did you guess?" joked Callum.

"Easy really, as I can't tell you apart," replied Clem.

"That's the giveaway, I suppose," agreed Callum light-heartedly.

"It sure is," replied Clem.

"So what trade are you?" asked Callum.

"Supply," replied Clem. "What about you?"

"Steward," answered Callum.

"Steward," seconded Calvin.

"Really? Wow!" piped up Stuart. "So am I," he added.

"Any idea what's happening with the training, as we haven't heard a thing?" asked Callum.

"Nope, we haven't got a clue either," replied Stuart, looking across at Clem.

"That's a mystery," said Callum.

"What's a mystery?" asked Stuart.

"That neither the supply trade trainees, or steward trade trainees know anything about their trade training arrangements," replied Callum.

"Oh, don't worry, something will turn up. We are at RAF Hereford, not RAF Swinderby. This is a lot more relaxed here. We've done all the discipline at our last posting, so let's enjoy a bit of leisure time, while we can," stated Clem.

"I don't know about you, but I want to get on in the Royal Air Force, and that means from day one, so if you're not keen to get started on a positive note, you're heading for trouble!" exclaimed Callum.

"I couldn't agree more, mate!" replied Clem.

"So why are you saying *RAF Hereford is not RAF Swinderby*?" asked Callum.

"Because it isn't, it's completely different. Take a look around and see for yourself. You'll see this is like chalk and cheese, compared to RAF Swinderby," replied Clem.

"Maybe you're right and it's me being stupid. Or perhaps I've still got my "Present Arms" head on, and think we'll be marching from pillar to post, like at RAF Swinderby," reflected Callum.

"Something like that bro, but we do need to find out what's happening, before it's too late," interrupted Calvin, in support of his twin brother Callum. "Or we may end up on a charge of AWOL!"

"Oh yes, I forgot about that," said Clem. "*This is the RAF, after all*."

"It is!" agreed Calvin.

"Come on then, let's take a walk to the Guardroom, and see if they have any information about the trade training, for the new intake," suggested Clem.

"Now you're thinking on the same wave length as me!" enthused Callum.

"I'm not a skiver mate, honestly, I've also signed up to learn a trade!" replied Clem.

As Clem and the other three airmen turned to go outside, and prepared to make their way to the Guardroom, the billet was suddenly filled with chatter, as two Non Commissioned Officers appeared out of nowhere.

"Good morning airmen!" called one of the NCO corporals, with a distinctive Irish twang.

Clem, Stuart, Callum and Calvin looked on in disbelief.

"Morning corporal!" replied Clem politely.

"Who's supply, and who's stewards?" questioned the Irish corporal.

"I'm supply, and these three are stewards," replied Clem.

"Okay, thanks, but where are the rest of the intake?" asked the Irish corporal.

"They're at breakfast, corporal," replied Clem.

"Breakfast, breakfast? You lot get breakfast too?" joked the Irish corporal.

"Yes corporal, but they shouldn't be too long," replied Clem.

"Okay fine. Well, my name's Corporal McCauley, and I'm the instructor for supply training," stated the Irish corporal, introducing himself.

"My name's Clem Harrison," was Clem's reply.

"I'm pleased to meet you Clem! *Have you eaten breakfast?*" asked Corporal McCauley.

"Yes corporal, half an hour ago. I'm an early riser," replied Clem.

"Good man, good man! We all waste far too much time sleeping and slumbering in bed! Life is for living, not for sleeping and dozing!" exclaimed Corporal McCauley.

"That's true, corporal," agreed Clem wholeheartedly.

A couple of minutes later, the billet was filled with boisterous banter and copious amounts of kerfuffle, as a dozen airmen made their way inside the building.

"Good *afternoon*!" called Corporal McCauley sarcastically. "Where have you all been?"

There was no reply.

"Has the cat got your tongue?" joked Corporal McCauley. Yet again, there was no reply.

"I take it that the cat has indeed got all of your tongues! Anyway, my name's Corporal McCauley, and I'm the instructor for supply training. Do we have any supply trade trainees among you?" he asked.

Six of the twelve airmen that had just appeared, put their hands up.

"Very good, we are getting somewhere now! That's seven, including Clem Harrison," stated Corporal McCauley happily.

Two minutes later, there was further commotion, as more airmen that lived in the upstairs part of the billet, appeared in front of Corporal McCauley.

"Come on in chaps, and welcome to the party!" exclaimed Corporal McCauley. "Do we have any supply trade trainees present among you?"

Another six airmen raised their hands.

"That's thirteen I make it, but I'm still one short. Are there any more supply trade trainees here?" asked Corporal McCauley.

"Yes corporal, me!" piped up a faint voice at the back, in all of a panic.

"Come along, where have you been?" replied Corporal McCauley.

"For breakfast, corporal," answered the faint voiced airman.

"Okay, well get fell in with the others, and don't be late tomorrow!" ordered Corporal McCauley.

"Okay corporal, sorry!" replied the faint voiced airman.

The fourteen supply trade trainees, including Clem, waited with bated breath, for their next instructions.

"Follow me airmen, and we shall proceed to the training block," ordered Corporal McCauley, leading the way towards the outside of the billet.

The fourteen airmen strolled leisurely outside, and Clem wondered whether the "Present Arms" and drill instruction learnt at RAF Swinderby, would ever be needed again.

Nobody questioned Corporal McCauley's relaxed attitude, as it was a breath of fresh air, after the hardship and dire discipline of RAF Swinderby.

They arrived at the training block ten minutes later, which was a flat roofed grey building, built with large bricks and pointed neatly with clean, white cement. It was a smart looking construction, which hardly looked its age, and must have been pre-Second World War.

"Find yourself a seat, and make yourself at home," stated Corporal McCauley. "There should be enough chairs and tables to go around," he added.

Clem pulled out a chair, and sat down on the left hand side of the room. He was keen and eager to get started and learn, and was relieved to have finally arrived at the trade training venue, after the worry of not hearing anything earlier. His mind was open, his ears were keen, and his head was ready to take everything on board.

"Now, I know this is your first full day here at Royal Air Force Hereford, but let me get some things straight, before we start the training," began Corporal McCauley.

Clem, and the rest of the supply trade trainees, listened carefully to what Corporal McCauley was going to say next.

"I expect punctuality at all times. So if you don't know what the word means, look it up in a dictionary. As well as punctuality, I expect each airman to work hard at the tasks that I set, and if needs be, doing homework in your own time, if you are struggling with a subject that we have covered during the day. If you are not prepared to do this, you and I will not get on very well, as I demand perfection. Now, this morning there was a ninety nine per cent failing from this intake, with regard to time-keeping, meaning that I was hanging around waiting for ninety nine per cent of my students to arrive. I will not tolerate this failing again. If it happens once more, you're out!" stated Corporal McCauley sternly.

The corporal stopped to catch his breath.

"Sleeping is over rated. We sleep for far too long in our life time, so I suggest to you all to invest in an alarm clock, set it half an hour ahead, and get up on the chimes of the alarm, to make yourself half an hour early, for training. That will suit me down to the ground, and get you in my "good books." That's all I wish to say. So, if you take these things on board, this training course will run as smoothly as silk!" exclaimed Corporal McCauley.

"But corporal, we didn't have any information on what time we were supposed to start," replied a stout built, Scottish speaking airman, with a bald head and freckles.

"Everything was detailed for you in the Guardroom. All you had to do was ask," explained Corporal McCauley.

The freckle faced Scotsman shook his head with indifference.

"Resources and Initiative taught you how to survive in Sherwood Forest, whilst at RAF Swinderby. If you'd used Resources and Initiative in this situation, you would have discovered the time and the place of your training course, without any problem!" exclaimed Corporal McCauley.

Nothing more was said by anybody. The matter was closed. The airmen knew where they stood, with regard to time-keeping, and Corporal McCauley was happy he had made his point, in a subtle and relaxed manner.

"Now, on to the course. This will be carried out in two stages. Theory and practical. The theory shall be conducted inside the classroom here, whilst the practical shall be carried out in a workshop, inside an hangar, close by. We shall go through the theory first, and cover all the neccessary points that you will need for the practical side of the training. Everything we cover in the classroom, regarding theory, will also be covered in the hangar, but will be on a practical basis in there. Are there any questions?" asked Corporal McCauley.

There wasn't any. The airmen were happy with what they had heard. It was all straight forward, and simple enough to understand.

"Good, good. That's what I like to hear. So before we get started, I shall roll call your name, and when I do, shout out to confirm your attendance, for marking," stated Corporal McCauley, brightly and confidently.

"Peter Bird," called Corporal McCauley.

"Yes corporal," replied the faint voiced airman from earlier, who had arrived late, and was fondly known to his family and friends, as "Squeaky" Bird.

"Gordon Bottle," shouted Corporal McCauley.

"Present, corporal," answered the airman, known to his mates back home as Gordon "Gin" Bottle.

"John Carter," yelled Corporal McCauley.

"Here corporal," replied the airman.

"Paul Craven," called Corporal McCauley.

"Yes, corporal," replied the airman.

"Clem Harrison," shouted Corporal McCauley.

"I'm here, corporal," replied Clem.

"Daniel MacJames," shouted Corporal McCauley.

"Yes corporal, over here," replied the bald headed, stout built, freckle faced Scotsman, who had earlier questioned the corporal's training arrangements.

"Luke Jappy," called Corporal McCauley.

"Yes, present corporal," replied the Aberdonian, with a broad Scottish twang.

"Gerry Joseph," shouted Corporal McCauley.

"I'm present, corporal," replied the airman.

"Alf King," called Corporal McCauley.

"Here, corporal," replied the airman.

"Jack Pott," yelled Corporal McCauley, looking twice at the name on his list.

"Yes corporal," replied the airman with the hilarious name, speaking in an Irish accent.

"Simon Roberts," bellowed Corporal McCauley.

"Yes, I'm here," replied the airman, in a broad Welsh accent.

"Norman Shepherd," shouted Corporal McCauley.

"Yes indeed, corporal," replied the airman confidently.

"Noah Williams," yelled Corporal McCauley.

"Here corporal," replied the airman, with a slight hint of a Welsh accent.

"Abraham Wray," called Corporal McCauley.

"Yes, I'm here corporal," replied the airman.

"Very good, you're all here, I didn't manage to scare anyone off! Better luck next time for me, tomorrow. Or maybe some will fall by the wayside, themselves!" joked Corporal McCauley, with a wicked sense of humour.

Most of the airmen were unsure what to make of Corporal McCauley, but they realised he was an experienced supply training instructor, and was not a man to mess with, as he mixed discipline with a wacky sense of humour, which most of the airmen on the training course reckoned had seen him through good times and bad, during his stint at RAF Hereford. As a group, they decided it would be best to knuckle down to some hard work, and do their best. Clem Harrison could see that there was a fair but strict man, standing at the front of the classroom, and Clem would do all he could to come through this trade training with flying colours. To do anything else would be foolhardy, and a complete waste of time, reckoned Clem.

"Okay, let's see if anyone has any hobbies, outside of work. I think hobbies are a great way to unwind and help take the pressure off, after a stressful and taxing day. So, hands up if anyone has a hobby," requested Corporal

McCauley, looking around at the fourteen airmen sitting at their desks, with blank expressions on their faces.

"Come on chaps, there must be somebody brave enough to admit to having an hobby!" exclaimed Corporal McCauley. "I know, I shall tell you my hobby. It's long distance running, that I participate in, each and every day, hence my point earlier about sleeping too much in the morning. I'm on the road at five thirty am, including Sunday!" exclaimed Corporal McCauley.

Clem Harrison was impressed with that.

"I've got a hobby, corporal," stated Clem courageously.

"What is it?" asked Corporal McCauley.

"Writing stories," replied Clem proudly.

The answer that Clem provided stunned the other trainees into silence.

"What sort of stories do you write?" asked Corporal McCauley.

"All sorts, really," replied Clem. "Mystery, thrillers and sport, to name a few," he added.

"Very good. What do you get out of writing?" asked Corporal McCauley.

"Relaxation, peace of mind, enjoyment, a sense of purpose, and it's something I really like doing," replied Clem.

"Yes, I can see where you're coming from with regard to all that, as I have the same experiences with my running. Good, good, thanks. Erm, is it Clem?" asked Corporal McCauley.

"Yes, corporal," replied Clem.

"Good, thanks Clem," reiterated Corporal McCauley, looking around the rest of the trainees sitting in front of him, and they were still looking blank in expression. "So, do we have any more hobbies, that you care to share with us?" added the corporal.

"I have a hobby," piped up Daniel MacJames, with a nervous snigger.

"Oh, do you, what is it?" asked Corporal McCauley.

"Drinking," replied Daniel, with tongue in cheek.

"I'm not sure you can call that *a hobby*," corrected Corporal McCauley, with half a smile.

"It is when it's connected to the other bits," replied Daniel.

"And what are the other bits?" asked Corporal McCauley.

"Darts and snooker!" exclaimed Daniel, in reply.

"That's fair enough, they're classed as hobbies. But I'm not sure about *the drinking*!" stated Corporal McCauley.

"Well, *without the drinking*, I'm rubbish at darts and snooker, and can only play when I've had a skinful of ale!" replied Daniel jovially.

The classroom full of trade trainees burst into laughter at that funny quip from the Scotsman, and it broke the ice among the airmen, and helped them settle down to their new surroundings. Corporal McCauley did not reply, but merely moved on to see if any other trainees had a hobby to share.

"I've got a hobby," piped up Peter Bird.

"Oh, have you, what's your hobby?" asked Corporal McCauley.

"I keep pigeons, and budgies," replied Peter.

"Do you really? And what benefit do you get out of that?" asked Corporal McCauley.

"Well, I race the pigeons for fun, and get great enjoyment out of it, and I breed budgies, and earn a little pocket money, when I sell them on," explained Peter.

"Very good, so it's a profitable hobby then?" asked Corporal McCauley.

"It's not the money I do it for, just the fun. It's something I really enjoy doing, and it's very relaxing," replied Peter.

"Good, good. As long as you enjoy it, that's all that counts," stated Corporal McCauley.

The corporal looked around at the faces of the rest of the trainees, and wondered if anyone else had an hobby they wished to share. He was certain there would be more, but he did not push it.

"Now, the reason I asked for your hobbies and interests, is because I believe keeping an active mindset is important, with maintaining a stable and happy attitude towards work. In the Royal Air Force, you shall have many opportunities to participate in sporting activities, such as football, cricket, rugby and tennis, and in many cases have time off from work to represent the station, where you are deployed. If any of you are sport orientated, you will see for yourself, if you are lucky enough, and good enough to be selected for a sports team. I, myself began my running career through competing for the Royal Air Force, and I have not looked back since. I have won many medals, certificates and trophies, and it has helped me with my working life, as it strengthened my mental and physical attributes. So, if you have a hobby, keep at it and enjoy, and give it everything you've got, because it's better than wasting time lazing and slumbering in your bed!" exclaimed Corporal McCauley.

"Before we get down to some serious work, does anyone have any questions for me, however mundane?" asked Corporal McCauley, looking around at the fourteen airmen, that were still wearing blank expressions on their faces.

There were a few shrugs of the shoulders, a couple of shakes of the head, and the rest remained expressionless, and seemed to be wondering what on earth was going to happen next.

"Has the cat *still got your tongues*?" asked Corporal McCauley. "I asked you if you had any questions. Is that a yes, or a no?" added the corporal, with a frown.

"No corporal," was the reply from all fourteen airmen, in unison.

"That's better, thankyou. It didn't hurt to be polite, did it? When I ask a question in future, I would like a response. Either a "yes corporal," or a "no corporal." Is that understood?" demanded Corporal McCauley.

"Yes corporal!" replied the fourteen airmen, in unison again.

"Good, good. We are getting somewhere, now," stated Corporal McCauley.

The corporal looked around the classroom for a volunteer, to assist him in handing out the workbooks, to each of the airmen. He picked the airman closest to him.

"Luke Jappy," called Corporal McCauley.

"Yes corporal?" replied a startled Luke Jappy, who jumped out of his skin, on the calling of his name.

"Sorry, did I wake you up, Jappy?" asked Corporal McCauley.

"No corporal, I'm fine," replied Luke Jappy.

"Okay, will you help me with these workbooks. If you take seven and hand them out, I shall distribute seven, and don't forget to keep one for yourself," instructed Corporal McCauley.

"Yes corporal," replied Luke Jappy, taking the seven workbooks, and instantly dropping them all over the floor.

"Are you sure you're awake, Jappy?" asked Corporal McCauley.

"Yes corporal, I'm absolutely fine," replied Luke Jappy.
The corporal handed out seven workbooks to the airmen sitting on the left hand side of the classroom, and he was dismayed to discover Luke Jappy was handing out a workbook to the same people.

"No Jappy! I've already handed out a workbook to those, can't you see? You concentrate on the right hand side of the classroom, and hand out a workbook to those guys," instructed Corporal McCauley.

"Sorry corporal, my mistake," stated Luke Jappy, turning to face the seven that were without the workbooks. He scratched his head, and tried to work out what was left and what was right, and he got himself into a complete muddle.

"What's up Jappy?" asked Corporal McCauley.

"I'm not sure if you meant the right hand side, from this direction," replied Luke Jappy, looking at the airmen from the front of the class. "Or that direction," he added, turning to face the blackboard, where Corporal McCauley was standing.

"Oh my word! Can't you see who's got a workbook, and who hasn't? Just hand out the books to those without, for goodness sake! Slap Happy Jappy!" yelled Corporal McCauley, jovially.

The other airmen that were sitting down, erupted into howls of laughter at that quip from the corporal, as they watched Luke Jappy turn crimson red in the face.

"Okay, okay, calm down, airmen, please!" shouted Corporal McCauley, loudly. "Has everyone got a workbook?" added the corporal, looking around at the fourteen airmen sitting down in front of him, each of them still sniggering at Luke Jappy's antics, and also at the quip from Corporal McCauley.

"Yes corporal!" replied the airmen in unison, eventually pulling themselves together.

"Good, good, we have lift off! Let's begin the course, then," suggested Corporal McCauley coolly, and clearing his throat. He took a gulp of cold water from the cup that was sitting on his desk, and prepared to begin the supply training course. Clem looked down at his workbook, and was ready to learn a brand new trade, courtesy of the Royal Air Force, and he was excited, keen and eager to get going.

"Please turn to page one, of your workbooks," commanded Corporal McCauley.

The airmen followed the instructions to a tee, and the room was filled with the noise of flicking paper being turned over, all at the same time.

"Welcome to the supply training course! The duration of this should be six weeks, although in some cases it could be longer, depending on how you negotiate the twists and turns of the tasks, and whether or not you pass the tests that are set. If you concentrate at all times, and don't let your mind wander, you should be alright. But remember, whatever you get out of this course depends on whatever you put into it," stated Corporal McCauley seriously, and sternly.

The airmen remained quiet, as they waited with bated breath to find out what was going to happen next. Clem reckoned things were going well, so far. But he did not let up on the concentration, and he continued to listen and learn, paying attention like he had never done before, in his life.

"We have a Voucher System here in the Royal Air Force, for the Supply Squadron, and they are in a booklet type form, which have a facility for tearing out the copies, for the different departments. Copy One is the top copy, Copy Two is the second copy and Copy Three is, yes, you've got it, the third copy. Copy One is sent to the Supply Control And Accounting Flight, otherwise known as SCAAF, for short, for admin purposes, Copy Two is retained by the Supplier for their records, which can be for example, the Electronic Stores Group, the Technical Stores, Petrol Oils and Lubricants or the Clothing Stores, and Copy Three is despatched with the goods to the department that ordered the part, for their records. It's simple stuff really, and once you get the hang of it, it's like a walk in the park, or for me, like a run in the park!" quipped Corporal McCauley.

There was a short pause by Corporal McCauley, as he waited for the airmen to take in everything he had said.

"Luke Jappy, where does Copy One go?" asked Corporal McCauley.

"It's sent to the Supply Control And Accounting Flight, otherwise known as SCAAF," replied Luke Jappy.

"Correct, well done, and Jappy, *why is it sent there*?" asked Corporal McCauley.

"For admin purposes," replied Luke Jappy.

"Correct, Jappy, well done!" enthused Corporal McCauley.

Luke Jappy beamed proudly like a beacon, at correctly answering two questions on the trot, after his earlier mistakes, with the workbooks.

"Daniel MacJames, where does Copy Two go?" asked Corporal McCauley.

"It's retained by the Supplier, for their records," replied Daniel MacJames.

"Correct, well done, and MacJames, *give me an example of a Supplier*?" asked Corporal McCauley.

"The Electronic Stores Group," replied Daniel MacJames.

"Correct MacJames, well done!" enthused Corporal McCauley.

"And Clem Harrison, *where does Copy Three go*?" asked Corporal McCauley.

"It's despatched to the department that ordered the item, along with the goods," replied Clem Harrison.

"Correct Harrison, well done!" enthused Corporal McCauley.

The corporal picked up his cup of cold water, and took another long gulp of the refreshing drink, and then calmly gathered his thoughts together.

"I told you it was simple stuff, well done to you Jappy, MacJames and Harrison. Now, moving swiftly on to the next stage. The Voucher has a location written at the top of the left hand side of the page, which is printed on all three copies. The location differs for each department. So, say it's the Electronic Stores Group, for instance, it'll have an E in a capital letter, to denote that department, and it's followed by a number for the aisle, followed by another letter in lower case, to indicate the exact shelf location, or in some cases a container bin, if the items are small, such as nuts, screws and nails," explained Corporal McCauley.

Clem took notes and jotted them down in his workbook. It was imperative he did this, as he knew it would be impossible for him to remember everything, so the copious amounts of information he wrote down would help him jog his memory, when it came to revising for any tests, in the future. It was a wise thing to do, reckoned Clem, although it gave him writer's cramp, but he knew a little suffering would be worth it, if he passed with flying colours.

"Peter Bird, where is the location situated on the Voucher?" asked Corporal McCauley.

"On the left hand side, corporal," replied Peter Bird.

"Correct, well done, and Bird, *is it at the top or the bottom of the Voucher*?" asked Corporal McCauley.

"At the top, corporal," replied Peter Bird.

"Correct Bird, well done!" enthused Corporal McCauley.

"Gordon Bottle, how many copies are the locations printed on?" asked Corporal McCauley.

"All three, corporal," replied Gordon Bottle.

"Correct, well done, and Bottle, *what's the letter for the Electronic Stores Group, that's written on the Voucher in a capital letter*?" asked Corporal McCauley.

"It's a capital E, corporal," replied Gordon Bottle.

"Correct Bottle, well done!" enthused Corporal McCauley.

"Jack Pott, how is the aisle location identified?" asked Corporal McCauley.

"It's written in number form," replied Jack Pott.

"Correct, well done, and Pott, *how is the shelf location identified*?" asked Corporal McCauley.

"In a letter form, corporal, in lower case," replied Jack Pott.

"Correct Pott, well done!" enthused Corporal McCauley.

"Clem Harrison, *what is stored in the container bins*?" asked Corporal McCauley.

"Small items, such as nuts, screws and nails, corporal," replied Clem Harrison.

"Correct Harrison, well done!" enthused Corporal McCauley.

There was another short pause, as Corporal McCauley had a swig from his cup of water, and he let the information sink into the heads of the airmen, as everyone would benefit from the question and answer session. It was Corporal McCauley's intention to get every airman through this course, without having to be back-flighted.

"Now, as well as the individual stores, such as the Electronic Stores Group, Petrol Oils and Lubricants, Technical Stores and Clothing Stores, where you may be working, there is also the R and D, or Receipt and Despatch Flight, to give it its full name," stated Corporal McCauley, pausing for breath. "This is where all the goods are received for the particular station, where you will be based in the future. Although sometimes, there are occasions when you forward on items to other smaller RAF stations nearby, that do not have an official delivery, and their goods are transported separately by the larger RAF station that receives it. But you'll hear more about that, when you get to your posting, as it doesn't affect everybody. Now, some of the deliveries received are early, and are widely known as the "Early Bird" delivery, and can be as early as four o'clock in the morning, in some cases. Although if that is the case, your shift runs from four am to twelve noon, meaning that you have the afternoon off! Now, the R and D department is a tight run ship, which means they need quick, efficient working practices, because there may be aircraft parts that are required by the Engineering and Electrical Squadrons urgently, to get the aeroplanes back into the air. So don't faff about, get the job done, and the parts checked off. Time is of the essence!" exclaimed Corporal McCauley, looking at his watch. "Are there any questions?"

"No corporal," replied the airmen, together in unison.

"Okay, go for a quick tea break, and be back here in fifteen minutes," ordered the corporal.

Clem sunk a lukewarm drink of tea down his throat, in next to no time, which he bought from the vending machine, in a corridor next to the classroom. He was gagging for a cuppa, and didn't know whether that was because it was warm in the classroom, or nerves. It was a bit of both, he reckoned. He looked around the place and could see the others in his training group had done exactly the same thing. So maybe they were as thirsty, and as nervous as him. There wasn't much noise coming from the airmen, except for Luke Jappy and Daniel MacJames having a heated conversation in their broad Scottish accents, about football.

"We're gonna kick your butts man!" exclaimed Luke Jappy.

"Nay man, I think you'll find it'll be the other way around. We shall knock your lot for six!" replied Daniel MacJames.

Clem couldn't help listening to the conversation, as it echoed up and down the corridor, but he didn't know what teams they were talking about.

"We're definitely gonna kick your butts, man. I told yer before and I'll say it again!" exclaimed Luke Jappy.

"Put your money where your mouth is!" replied Daniel MacJames.

"You're on, I'll bet you a tenner we take all the points on January nineteenth!" said Luke Jappy bravely.

"Raise it to twenty, and I might be interested!" replied Daniel MacJames.

"Okay man, twenty it is!" agreed Luke Jappy. "Come on the Dons!" he added.

"Come on the 'Gers!" replied Daniel MacJames, shaking Luke Jappy by the hand, to confirm the £20 bet.

Clem worked out the teams, and reckoned it was Aberdeen and Glasgow Rangers. He would keep an eye out for the score when the game was played in mid January. He had no idea who were the best between the two teams, as he had not been paying much attention to the Scottish football scene, but it didn't dampen his enthusiasm, especially after the heated discussion between Luke Jappy and Daniel MacJames.

Ten minutes later, Corporal McCauley came through into the corridor, and beckoned the airmen back into the classroom.

"Come on guys, tea break's over. It's back to the grindstone," ordered Corporal McCauley lightheartedly.

The airmen drifted slowly back into the classroom, and settled back in their chairs, and were ready to resume with the trade training programme.

"Don't get yourselves too comfortable, as you're all off outside in a minute," stated Corporal McCauley.

Clem and the other trainees looked nervously at each other, wondering what was going to happen in the next stage of the course. It was a daunting thought, but Clem put on a brave face.

"Okay, if you're all ready, follow me! There are three departments involved in this, so I shall split you into two groups of five, and one group of four, seeing as there are fourteen of you," stated Corporal McCauley.

The airmen followed Corporal McCauley out of the classroom and they entered a large, cold hangar that backed onto the trade training building.

"Jappy, MacJames, King, Shepherd and Joseph, you're group one. Bird, Bottle, Harrison, Roberts and Williams, are group two. Pott, Craven, Carter and Wray are group three," ordered Corporal McCauley. "Will you line up outside the room number that corresponds to the group number, that I have just given you, please," he added.

The airmen quickly shuffled into their places, which were either in front of room 1, room 2, or room 3, that were situated in a row, on the edge of the large, cold hangar.

"This exercise is designed for role-play purposes, on the practical skills side of the job, that you will need to carry out in a satisfactory manner, in order to continue to move forward with your career, in the Royal Air Force. Room One is Supply Control And Accounting Flight, otherwise known as SCAAF," began Corporal McCauley, in a loud, clear voice. "Room Two is the Technical Stores, and Room Three is the department that ordered the goods. Now, you were all brilliant with the theory side of things in the classroom, so let's see what you're like in practice. Don't forget where you are when you enter the room, and think on your feet! Practical is just as simple as theory, so for goodness sake, have your thinking caps on!" exclaimed Corporal McCauley.

Clem swallowed hard and looked at the door. It read "Technical Stores," and he struggled to remember what copy of the Voucher went there. His mind had gone blank. He revisited the classroom in his head, and recalled Copy One as SCAAF, Copy Two as Electronic Stores Group, Technical Stores, Petrol Oils and Lubricants and Clothing Stores, and Copy Three as the receiver of the goods, and he repeated this in his mind, over and over again. But he did not feel comfortable. He began to panic, and fought hard to maintain his composure, by continuing to repeat the process of where Copy One went, who received Copy Two, and what happened to Copy Three, and when the doors of the three rooms were opened, he remained as cool, calm and collected as he possibly could, but in reality, he was a bag of nerves.

Clem waited his turn, as he was third in the queue, after Peter Bird and Gordon Bottle, and the door was slammed shut after Peter Bird went in, with no chance of clues for any of the awaiting trainees. It just added to the tension, that they were already feeling. Clem was trying hard to be composed, but he was struggling. He watched Peter Bird leave Room Two, and he glanced at Gordon Bottle going in. Clem was next, and his heart was thudding like a drum. The door slammed shut after Gordon Bottle, leaving Clem again with no opportunity to listen in, and pick up some vital tips, and Peter Bird was no good for advice, as no sooner had he arrived, he was quickly whisked away again to the next room, by a very watchful Corporal McCauley, who had his eyes on everyone, and was taking notes for the student dossiers. It was not long before Gordon Bottle came through the door of Room Two, leaving Clem free to make his way inside, for his first taste of practical trade training, and it did not go too well, from the start.

Clem went to pot. His thought processes went haywire, and he could not think straight. It was a complete disaster, and Clem wanted the ground to swallow him up, there and then.

"What copy of the Voucher does the Technical Stores keep, when an item is despatched?" asked the pipe smoking grey haired elderly man, of around 70 years of age, holding up three copies of the Voucher, Copy One, Copy Two and Copy Three.

"Erm, Copy, Copy...." stuttered Clem, with doubt in his tone, unable to remember anything in his head. He struggled to recall his own name, at that precise moment, and played for time to make himself less conspicuous. But it only seemed to make things worse, as the elderly man with the strong tobacco in his pipe, was less than understanding, and was becoming a little impatient. But all Clem could smell was the smoke billowing out of the elderly man's black pipe, which had the aroma of being St Bruno Flake tobacco.

"Well?" asked the elderly man.

"Erm, Copy, Copy Two?" guessed Clem, in a blind panic.

"Yes, correct! That was a lucky guess, wasn't it?" replied the elderly grey haired man, with the black pipe.

Clem did not answer, and could not wait to get out of the room, to collect his thoughts. He nodded his head in agreement, turned round to face the door, and then quickly dashed outside into the open air, in an attempt to clear his foggy mind, after the embarrassment of being tongue-tied, and also to remove the stifling aroma from his nostrils of the St Bruno Flake tobacco smoke, that was pouring out of the elderly man's pipe. He had never suffered from brain fog before, and had to admit to himself that it was a weird experience, as the pressure mounted up, with each tick of the clock, on the wall of the room, and echoed all around his head. The longer Clem had delayed his answer, the worse it became for him. He did not fancy going through that again.

As soon as Clem got through the door, that slammed shut on his exit, he felt a whole lot better. Whether it had been nerves, laziness, panic, brain fog or smoke inhalation, from the elderly man's black pipe, Clem did not know. But whatever it was, it was something that taught him a lesson, in assertiveness. He needed to learn how to handle the pressure situation, of a practical assessment, as this exercise had taught him how little he knew about himself.

"Clem Harrison, *have you been in Room Two*?" asked Corporal McCauley.

"Yes, corporal," replied Clem.

"Okay, wait your turn outside Room Three, then, please," answered Corporal McCauley.

"Yes, will do, corporal," replied Clem feeling a little better in himself. He was hoping with all his might that there were no pipes, cigars or cigarette smokers in this room, and he headed for the door marked "Three."

Clem waited in line, after Alf King and Norman Shepherd. He watched Daniel MacJames leave the room, and waited for the door to slam shut like the other one did, and he was not disappointed, although it appeared to close quicker and louder than the door in Room Two.

Clem went through the same routine with regards to the Vouchers, but did not overthink this time. He relaxed, took long deep breaths and learnt his lesson from earlier. This was Room Three, where the Voucher is issued with the goods, was easy enough to remember, and Clem was happy he would not mess it up like he did with the Copy Two response. Receipt and Despatch was all he needed to provide as his answer.

Alf King came out of Room Three and Norman Shepherd went in. Clem was next. It wasn't long before it was his chance to make amends, by answering the question, without delay. He continued not to overthink, and he did not panic. The lesson from Room Two had been well and truly learnt.

When Norman Shepherd came through the door after spending a couple of minutes inside there, it was Clem's turn. He breezed confidently inside and was cool, calm and collected.

"What is this department called?" asked another grey haired elderly man with a pipe, which billowed smoke like a chimney, and smelled exactly the same as the other elderly grey haired man's pipe tobacco.

"Receipt and Despatch," replied Clem.

"Correct, well done young man. And what copy of the Voucher does Receipt and Despatch receive, Copy One, Copy Two or Copy Three?" asked the pipe smoking grey haired old man.

"Copy Three," replied Clem.

"Correct, well done," answered the elderly man.

Clem was in no rush to leave the room this time, as he felt good and had answered quickly and correctly, and he stayed rooted to the spot.

"*Was there anything else?*" asked the elderly man impatiently.

"No, no, I'm fine," replied Clem.

"Off you go then, young man," stated the elderly man, puffing billow after billow a series of numerous clouds of strong smoke, from his pipe.

"Okay, thanks," replied Clem, and he turned to leave the room. When he reached the door, he turned to glance at the old bloke, and could have sworn it was the same fellow from Room Two.

When Clem reached the fresh air of the spacious hangar outside, he beamed proudly to himself, over his assertiveness and confidence with the latest practical test, and was approached by Corporal McCauley.

"Okay Clem, you need to wait outside Room One next, please," stated Corporal McCauley efficiently.

"Yes corporal," replied Clem.

When Clem arrived at the door marked "Room One", he joined the queue that consisted of Simon Roberts and Noah Williams. They went and came within a few minutes, and it left Clem at the head of the queue. This was Room One, which meant Copy One of the Voucher, that was issued to SCAAF.

Clem entered the room and looked for an elderly grey haired man with a pipe, and he was not disappointed. The guy sitting behind the desk was hidden in a cloud of smoke, which Clem reckoned was the old favourite, St Bruno Flake. Clem had to look twice before he believed his eyes, as the man sitting down behind the brown desk, was the spitting image of the other two fellows in Room Two and Room Three.

"What copy of the Voucher is issued to SCAAF?" asked the pipe smoking old man.

"Copy One," replied Clem.

"Correct young man, and what does SCAAF stand for?" asked the old man.

"Supply Control And Accounting Flight," replied Clem.

"Yes, correct young man, well done," stated the old man.

"Thank you," replied Clem, and he quickly turned round to depart outside. He was pleased with himself for keeping his nerve, and except for a little hesitation in Room Two, it would have been a perfect result, but Clem realised he was growing and developing as a person, and learning all the time.

Corporal McCauley looked around at the trainees, to check on their progress in the practical exercises.

"Has everyone had a chance to test their knowledge of the supply theory training, with practical experience in the three rooms?" asked Corporal McCauley, in a loud, booming voice.

"Yes corporal!" replied the fourteen trade trainees, together in unison, in an equally resounding tone.

"Very good! I shall gather your results in due course, from the assessors, and the results shall go with you to your permanent posting, after the training is fully completed. Don't worry about these little tests. They are designed *to help you, and to help us*, at the same time. We have to find out whether you're round pegs in square holes, and the only way to do this is by small, practical exams. This training course will be full of these, in various guises, and each will have a contributory factor to play in your future career," stated Corporal McCauley, slowly and clearly.

The airmen took on board what was being said, and they were all reasonably happy with what they had encountered, in the three rooms. It was basic and simple stuff, and only Clem had been found to struggle with remembering the facts and figures in the earlier stages, but he had redeemed himself after his shaky start, and had gone on to show great promise, in the subsequent exams.

"Well, that takes care of the morning. Thank you very much guys for the great participation, and I hope you've enjoyed your first session at the RAF Hereford Supply Trade Training School. Take an hour for lunch, and be back here at one o'clock sharp. And listen guys, I mean one o'clock, not one minute past one!" shouted Corporal McCauley, clearly displaying that he was a stickler for perfect timekeeping.

"Yes corporal!" replied the fourteen airmen, together in unison.

"Off you go then, and enjoy your lunch!" called Corporal McCauley, loudly.

The airmen strolled briskly to the Airmen's Mess. Clem however, was not all that hungry, after his big breakfast, although he wasn't going to miss lunch. If brekkie was anything to go by, he was certainly looking forward again, to the fayre on offer, and he pledged to himself that he would somehow find room in his belly, for something to eat, this lunchtime.

Clem queued up outside, with the other supply trainees, and peering through the window, he noticed that there were many non RAF uniformed personnel present in the Airmen's Mess. He had no idea who they were, or what they were doing, and he did not ask any questions. But he did know that the Special Air Service, otherwise known as the SAS, were based here at RAF Hereford.

Once Clem was inside the warmth of the building, he noticed how quickly the queue was moving. He waited in the "hot carvery buffet" line that had a selection of roast meats, including beef, pork, lamb and turkey, and it looked just as good as any restaurant in a Five Star hotel. The smell of the food was fantastic and it made Clem's stomach rumble.

There was an old guy in front of him dressed in civilian clothing, and he looked to be in his mid to late sixties. Clem followed him in turn, as they both queued up for the carvery. The old man had two large slices of pork served on his plate by the chef, and then he shuffled along. Clem chose beef and he too shuffled along. The old man in front of Clem filled his plate up with a selection of garden peas, carrots, turnip, broccoli and succulent roast potatoes, from the self service counter, before walking off and pouring a runny brown substance all over his delicious food, from a large unmarked jug, that was sitting at the edge of the serving table. Clem had to look twice, as the old man had walked past the gravy pan, and had approached the puddings, and he appeared to have poured chocolate sauce all over his dinner, by mistake. Clem could not believe his eyes, and he made sure he did not make the same error, as he double checked with the chef where the gravy was located, after he had served himself a selection of vegetables, including carrots, peas, cabbage and broccoli.

"Is this the gravy?" asked Clem, pointing to a silver jug on the serving hatch.

"Yep, it sure is. *It's not the chocolate sauce, that's for sure*!" replied the chef, with a sense of humour.

"Cheers!" stated Clem, with a smirk.

If only the chef knew what the old man in the civilian clothes, queuing before Clem, had just done. That would have been a story for the chef to tell his mates down in the NAAFI bar, later that evening.

Clem poured a serving of gravy all over his delicious looking lunch, and loaded the plate with a dollop of mashed potato, for good measure. Somehow his appetite had returned.

Clem looked around the packed room for his mates, but he could not see any of them. The place was crammed full, and there didn't seem to be many spare places. Clem gave up looking for his colleagues, and made his way to the first available seat. He was amazed to discover his associates were sat on the next table, and he hadn't seen them. It was only when he got a tap on the shoulder from Alf King, that Clem had realised where they all were.

"You not sitting with us?" called Alf King, facetiously.

"Oh sorry, I didn't see you there," replied Clem, red faced with embarrassment.

"You didn't see us? We're on the next table to you!" replied Alf, jovially.

"Sorry, but I couldn't see you for looking!" answered Clem quickly.

Alf laughed heartily. He found that remark very funny.

"Never mind mate. I'll book you an appointment, with the RAF Hereford optician!" joked Alf.

"Good idea, I could do with one. My eyes are terrible!" agreed Clem, continuing with the banter, and spilling the gravy from his plate all over the table. It went everywhere.

"Steady on pal. Have you been on the beer?" piped up Gordon Bottle.

"Nope, the gin!" joked Clem, with tongue in cheek.

"Ha! *That's my nickname*!" replied Gordon.

"What, *gin*?" asked Clem.

"Yep, that's correct, after the alcoholic drink, *Gordon's Gin*!" replied Gordon.

"Ha! I like it. That's very funny!" answered Clem.

Clem mopped up the gravy with a couple of paper napkins that were lying loose on the table, and then he tucked keenly into his lunch. The pangs of hunger in his stomach were rife, and he was pleased he turned up here. This Royal Air Force food was getting better and better, thought Clem.

"Did anyone notice the three old men in those rooms, were spitting images of one another?" asked Alf King.

"Yep, I did!" agreed Clem, as he chewed eagerly on a mouthful of beef.

"I could hardly see them, for the smoke!" exclaimed Gordon "Gin" Bottle.

"Me too, to be honest!" agreed Alf, nodding his head.

"They must be keeping those tobacco companies in great profit, by the amount of pipe smoking they were doing!" piped up Jack Pott.

"That's true," agreed Clem.

"I think they were triplets!" stated Alf, out of the blue.

"You're joking!" exclaimed Clem.

"Hey, how did you know? *That's my middle name....Joe King*!" replied Alf.

"Ha! Really? You're Joe King!" exclaimed Clem.

"It's true," replied Alf. "My mother wanted to make Joe my first name, as she liked it that much. But my father said, don't be ridiculous, I'd have the mickey taken out of me, throughout my whole life. So they made Joe my middle name instead," he explained.

"Ha! First we have Gordon's Gin, and now we have Joe King! Whatever next?" stated Clem.

"Me! I'm known to my friends and family, as Peter "Squeaky" Bird!" piped up Peter Bird.

"Ha! That's funny too!" stated Clem loudly.

The airmen all guffawed and chortled together, at the revelations of the three trainees, in a light hearted, friendly manner, without showing any malice whatsoever.

"None of those beats mine though," piped up Jack Pott.

"Oh yes, Jack Pott! That's another good one. We've got a huge haul of nicknames here," stated Clem.

"Yes, *but Jack Pott is my real name though*," replied Jack.

"That makes it even funnier!" exclaimed Alf King.

"It's not as funny as mine!" piped up Luke Jappy. "Slap Happy Jappy!" he said loudly.

The supply trade trainees roared with laughter at Luke Jappy, and they remembered what Corporal McCauley had said in the classroom, which made it even funnier than the others.

Clem finished eating his lunch, and had to admit that it was better than it looked, and it looked great! He didn't bother to mention anything to his colleagues about the old man dressed in civilian clothing, that had poured chocolate sauce all over his roast pork and succulent vegetables. He decided the guy may have had a brain lapse, like he had suffered in Room One during the practical exercise, so he took pity on the old chap, and let it be.

Clem checked his watch and found it was half past twelve. He had thirty minutes to himself before he had to return to the training room. He decided it would be a good idea to buy a newspaper and find out what was happening in the world. It had been a whole day and a half since he had caught up with the news going on in the planet. He bought the Sun morning newspaper, but didn't find much to read. It was full of dull politics, which he had no real interest in. But the sports pages were informative, and they provided good reports on his two teams, Tottenham Hotspur and Aston Villa. And in other news, his home town club, Hull City had signed Billy Bremner from Leeds United, which was a breaking scoop, hot off the press.

Aston Villa had played Coventry City at home, in their latest match, and drew 2-2, whilst Tottenham Hotspur had a narrow 2-1 away defeat at Sunderland. Aston Villa were currently in fourth place in the English First Division, with twenty seven points from sixteen games, with Tottenham Hotspur languishing near the bottom of that division, in twentieth position, with fifteen points from sixteen games, and in real danger of relegation to Division Two.

Clem didn't think Tottenham Hotspur would go down. He hoped they continued with their fighting spirit, following their defeat at Sunderland, with a victory in their next game against Stoke City, on November 27th. Whilst Aston Villa were due to play Coventry City again, away on the same day. Clem awaited those two games with relish. But he was mostly looking forward to when Aston Villa played Tottenham Hotspur on 20th April, and again on 30th April. As those games meant he couldn't lose, because whoever won the matches, meant one of his favourite teams had been victorious. Although with Tottenham Hotspur's current plight at the foot of the table, he was hoping they would somehow claw themselves out of trouble, with two vital wins against Aston Villa, and then go on an unbeaten run, until the end of the season.

After browsing the rest of the sports pages, Clem put the newspaper away, and prepared to make his way to the training room. He hadn't thought any more of his mental blockage from Room One, and had promptly put it behind him. The incident with the old man and the chocolate sauce poured over his pork, roast potatoes and vegetables had taught him a lesson in never underestimating life. It was always springing up something challenging, no matter what location, or situation.

Clem looked around for the rest of the guys, after taking his head out of his newspaper, but there was no sign of them. He reckoned they must have been scared by Corporal McCauley's stern warning about not being late, even by one minute, so he made himself scarce, and made brisk tracks out of the Airmen's Mess, towards the supply training building. He looked at his watch, and it read 12.50 pm. He had ten minutes to get himself to the training room, which he estimated to be plenty of time.

Clem made it back to the supply training room, with only one minute to spare. It was a good job he moved when he did, as if he had continued reading his newspaper for two minutes longer, he would have had to face the wrath of an angry Corporal McCauley. Fortunately it didn't come to that, and everything was tickety-boo.
Clem looked around the room, and noticed there were two empty places. The chairs where Luke Jappy and Daniel MacJames had been sitting. Clem glanced at his watch and discovered it was one minute past one o'clock, the dreaded time that Corporal McCauley had warned everybody about. Two minutes later, the noisy Scottish pair arrived at the classroom, and were full of the joys of spring, without a care in the world. They entered the training room, and approached the places where they had been sitting earlier, without any mention of an apology to Corporal McCauley. It was rude behaviour, but the corporal ignored it this time. Although he noted it in his head, for later.
The room was suddenly filled with the sound of noisy chatter, laughter, banter and keen conversation between the fourteen airmen, as if the volume control had been instantly cranked up to its limit. Lunch had gone down

very well, and had perked up everyone to the extreme, resulting in this deafening and boisterous racket.

"Quiet now, please!" yelled Corporal McCauley. "If you don't mind!"

The trainees hushed instantly, and the room became so silent, it was possible to hear a pin drop.

"Did everyone enjoy their lunch?" asked Corporal McCauley.

"Yes corporal!" replied the airmen, loudly, in unison.

"Very good! I've heard the Airmen's Mess is serving up some pretty good nosh, at the moment," stated Corporal McCauley.

"Yes corporal, it is!" replied the airmen together.

"And it's *so delicious*, that some trainees are unable to leave the building, in order to obtain seconds," stated Corporal McCauley.

Clem swallowed hard, and remembered what he had done at breakfast time, when he went up twice for food, and had two helpings of the fry-up.

"Now, I don't mind you lot having two servings of grub. But when it's affecting your judgement in arriving to class on time, then it really starts to peeve me off! Do you understand what I'm saying, *Jappy and MacJames?*" demanded Corporal McCauley.

"Yes corporal!" replied Luke Jappy and Daniel MacJames, together in unison.

"Good, I'll say no more on the matter. But please don't be tempted to take root in the Airmen's Mess. You're not on holiday, this is a trade training course!" bellowed Corporal McCauley.

"Sorry corporal. We over indulged, and got sidetracked," explained Daniel MacJames.

"You're not the first, and I'm certain you won't be the last. Just make sure this will be the final time I have to lecture you. Because you know how the saying goes, three and you're out! Next time, it'll be your third warning for timekeeping, and believe me, you shall definitely be out!" bawled Corporal McCauley.

Clem gasped a huge sigh of relief, as he had expected a telling off too, but he realised he was in the clear this time, and he wiped the sweat from his brow.

The afternoon's training session commenced soon after, with the fourteen trainees concentrating hard on the tasks ahead. Each of them knowing that Corporal McCauley was taking no prisoners in his quest to train them up, displaying a ruthless and aggressive attitude, that was sugar coated by his eccentricity and sense of humour. But what the airmen now also realised, was that Corporal McCauley was no pushover, and not easily fooled by excuses. He had not become a champion long distance runner by being a pussycat and easy going. There was a streak of granite running right through the centre of this genial Irishman.

"Are there any questions about the training so far, however trivial? It doesn't matter how ridiculous the question is. If it's bugging you, get it out in the open!" demanded Corporal McCauley, with empathy.

There were no takers on this one. Clem was happy enough. He had come to terms with his ordeal in Room Two, and was looking to the future with optimism.

"No corporal," replied the airmen in unison.

"Okay, fair enough. Now, the Voucher System is a simplistic way to keep track of all the goods, that are in transit around the world. The three copies are designed for the departments to keep everything under control. And at the hub of this is the Supply Control And Accounting

Flight, which maintains everything in accordance with the rules and regulations of the Royal Air Force Supply Squadron. The Vouchers are produced by the Supply Control And Accounting Flight, otherwise known as SCAAF, and each department has a daily batch of Vouchers to clear as soon as possible," began Corporal McCauley. "In the Technical Stores Flight, for instance. The parts supplied range from small items such as nuts, bolts, screws and washers, to larger goods such as aircraft propellers, aircraft body panels and helicopter rotor blades. So you can see that the diversity goes from one extreme to the other," stated Corporal McCauley, enlightening the fourteen trainees, with his ample knowledge of the Technical Stores Flight. "Moving on to the Electronic Stores Group. This is a department that works in tandem with the Electronic Engineering Testing Department, that repairs the aircraft's electrical parts, such as the radios, flight instruments, switches, dials, altimeters, gyros, indicator panels, and so on," explained Corporal McCauley.

The trainees listened intently and with great intrigue, as they took on board what type of components the Electrical Supply Group dealt with, and they all jotted down notes in their exercise books.

"Moving on to the Clothing Store. This is simple enough to grasp, and it explains itself. It supplies everything the airman and airwoman needs in respect of uniform clothing, and equips the permanent personnel of its RAF station with uniform to wear, to maintain a high degree of smartness in the workforce. There are no excuses for any of you to look scruffy or shabby, with torn trousers, ripped shirts or scuffed shoes. A trip to the Clothing Store will put that right instantly. Once you've obtained a Voucher from either your Flight Sergeant, Sergeant or Corporal, you will be issued with new clothing, in exchange for the Voucher," explained Corporal McCauley coolly, calmly and collectedly. He paused for a short while, to take a swig of water from his cup.

"Now, that's three of the four main stores which are controlled by SCAAF, and Vouchers are produced for all four, to enable the airman or airwoman to process the transactions. The fourth store is Petrol Oils and Lubricants, otherwise known as POL, which among other things, works in tandem with the Bowsers Refuelling Department. Here, there is a slightly different set up for the supply of aviation fuel, *that is Voucher-free*. The bowser crew refuel the aircraft, and control the flow of the fuel issued. The Supply Squadron stores it in tanks, and refuels the bowsers, as and when required, but keep a record of the fuel in the tanks by means of *dipping the tanks with a dipstick*, where readings are noted on a wall chart, in the POL office, and they order the fuel in bulk delivery from the FINA company, based in Immingham," added the corporal. He refreshed his parched mouth with another swig from his cup of water.

"But the Petrol Oils and Lubricants stores *do have Vouchers* for the smaller items that are supplied, such as tinned compounds, polish, cleaning agents and other chemical products, where they are stored in outhouses, behind thick protective walls, for health and safety reasons. As they contain highly explosive materials," stated Corporal McCauley. "*And if any of you happen to be deployed in POL, you shall undergo an intensive two day training course in Liquid Oxygen handling, at RAF Cardington,*" he added, before taking a further gulp of water from his cup. "This Liquid Oxygen product otherwise known as LOX is stored outside, and cordoned off behind a secure wire fence, well away from office buildings and living quarters, because of its hazardous nature, where it's a danger to life and limb. The POL people in addition to all this, look after the various industrial gas and oxygen cylinders of numerous shapes and sizes, that are also stored outside in a large compound, but kept well away from the Liquid Oxygen storage location," added Corporal McCauley, with a smirk of irony in his expression.

Clem was fascinated with the subject, and didn't realise how many different aspects there were to the Supply Squadron. There were a multitude of departments that required varied skill sets, and Petrol Oils and Lubricants seemed to be the most fascinating of them all. And it appeared to be outside working too, which suited Clem, down to the ground. He didn't fancy being cooped up in an office, nor a storeroom, which ruled out the Technical Stores, Clothing Stores, SCAAF and the Electronic Stores Group. But Petrol Oils and Lubricants seemed ideal for him.

So, with Clem's mind made up about his future commitments to the Royal Air Force, and his choice of occupation in the Supply Squadron. He looked forward to the rest of the training course, with a deep sense of satisfaction, knowing full well what he wanted, and what his heart was set on, and it proved a welcome relief. All he had to do now was concentrate for six weeks, pass his exams, and obtain his first posting to his permanent RAF station, wherever that may be.

The rest of the afternoon was spent on theory, which Clem always found slightly dull, and Corporal McCauley recapped on the Voucher System, and in particular where each copy was sent, and he drilled this home time and time again, making it his number one priority for the fourteen trainees to completely grasp. He need not have worried, as the airmen fully understood this aspect of the supply training, including Clem, who put his panic attack in Room Two well behind him. But Corporal McCauley continued his stance on the revision, as this was his style, in a bid to maintain competence and excellence, within the group.

"I'm happy with your knowledge on theory. I'm just as ecstatic about your understanding on practical. But I need to find out if you can make it the Grand Slam, with these little gems!" teased Corporal McCauley, giving nothing away.

Clem and the other trainees groaned inwardly. They all wondered what Corporal McCauley had up his sleeve this time.

"Can anyone answer this, in a free-for-all?" began Corporal McCauley.

The airmen listened with eager ears.

"What does POL stand for?" asked the corporal.

"Petrol Oils and Lubricants!" replied Clem, as quick as a flash.

"Correct Clem, well done!" answered Corporal McCauley, preparing himself with another question to address the trainees. "What does the Technical Stores Flight hold?" he asked.

"Nuts, bolts, screws, rotor blades, propellers and aircraft body panels," replied Daniel MacJames instantly.

"Yes, correct Daniel, well done!" answered Corporal McCauley. "Now, who can tell me what the Electronic Stores Group holds?"

"Radios, switches, dials, altimeters and gyros," replied Alf King.

"Yes, correct Alf, well done," answered Corporal McCauley. "So, what do you need in order to obtain a shirt and a pair of trousers, from the Clothing Store?" asked the corporal.

"A Voucher!" replied Gordon Bottle.

"Yes, correct Gordon, well done," answered Corporal McCauley. He nodded with satisfaction at these impressive replies, and it reinforced his confidence in the trainees.

"Can anyone answer this question? What does LOX stand for?" asked Corporal McCauley.

"Liquid Oxygen!" replied Clem immediately.

"Yes Clem, another good answer, well done!" enthused Corporal McCauley. "And here's another one for you all. Where does the Liquid Oxygen two day training course take place?"

"RAF Cardington!" replied Clem, as keen as mustard.

"Correct Clem, you're quick today, well done!" answered Corporal McCauley, pausing for another sip of water from his cup. "So, on that positive note, I'm pleased to say this emphatically concludes day one's training, *with the Grand Slam*! Well done to you all! Enjoy your evening, and be back here at nine in the morning, *sharp*!" exclaimed Corporal McCauley, quickly ushering the fourteen trainees out of the room.

Clem ate his tea, and he wasn't sure how he had put it all away, and more worryingly where he had put it, as he was only a skinny ten stone weakling, at the best of times. But somehow he packed it into his slim frame without any problems at all. The evening meal tonight consisted of steak, chips and peas, with a cup of strong bromide-free tea, and apple crumble and custard for pudding. It was, as Clem would put it, "delicious as usual," and he couldn't wait for the next meal time, in the morning. This food was extremely moreish, he reckoned.

After eating his tea, Clem sat back in his chair and tried to reflect on his day, regathering in his head all the important points he had learned. But he gave up after a few seconds, as there were too many to think about.

"Who's up for a game of table football? We need four to play, two-a-side," piped up Alf King.

"I'll play," replied Clem keenly.

"Come on then, we need two more! Anyone else want to lark?" asked Alf.

"Yep, go on then," agreed Gordon Bottle.

"Anybody else interested?" asked Alf, in a pleading tone.

"Yep, me!" shouted Peter Bird.

"Okay, it's me and Clem, versus Gordon and Peter!" stated Alf bossily.

"That's fair enough! Are you ready for a good hiding?" replied Gordon facetiously.

"In your dreams!" answered Alf, with tongue in cheek.

"We are *the red team*!" insisted Gordon.

"Okay, okay, keep your hair on!" exclaimed Alf.

The game commenced, and Clem took control of the defence and goalkeeper, whilst Alf managed the forwards and midfield. In opposition, Gordon was in charge of the goalkeeper and defence, leaving Peter to operate the midfield and forward line. The game was fast and furious and the four players were quickly into action, and deep in concentration. Two goals were fired in swiftly by Peter Bird, giving Clem no chance in goal, and it looked distinctly to Clem that Peter "Squeaky" Bird had played this game before. Clem had played the game a few times at his former school's Youth Club, on an evening, but he wasn't as good as Peter "Squeaky" Bird. This guy was a proper whizz kid.

Two goals turned into three, and then four, before Alf looked at Clem with an expression of dismay on his face.

"*Have you played this game before?*" asked Alf, directing his question at Clem, with a baffled expression on his face.

"Yes, but not much though. Have you?" replied Clem.

"Yep, but I was mainly in defence though," answered Alf.

"Why didn't you say? As I've only played as a midfielder and striker!" revealed Clem.

"Let's swap over then!" exclaimed Alf.

"Okay, as I'm sure it can't get any worse," agreed Clem, shrugging his shoulders, with indifference.

"Come on, let's go for it!" exclaimed Alf positively.

Clem took hold of the two bars that controlled the attacking players and the midfield, and he had instant success, when he drilled the ball home into the back of the net, with a thunderous shot from the centre of the pitch, to get them off the mark, and making the score 4-1. Another long, hopeful shot, by Alf this time, from the defence, managed to evade every single player in front of him, and ended up in the back of the goal to bring the score even closer, at 4-2. The change of tactics used by Alf and Clem were suddenly working. "Squeaky" Bird didn't panic however, and used all his guile and skill to find the back of the net, with two cracking strikes, that brought the score to 6-2, still remaining in favour of Peter "Squeaky" Bird and Gordon Gin Bottle. Clem was having none of it, and didn't lay over and die. It only made him work even harder and play better, and with great support from Alf Joe King, they pulled three goals back, with some acute teamwork, and bamboozled their opponents with deft touches, crafty side steps and weaving from side to side, to bring the current score to a mouth watering 6-5. But still in favour of Peter "Squeaky" Bird and Gordon Gin Bottle. It was nip and tuck, and going down to the wire, and it brought beaming smiles of joy, ugly frowns of tension and loud groans of despair, with more goals, a few near misses, plenty of saves, and some superb action, in both penalty areas, as the two sides continued to lock horns and looking to turn the screw. Alf scored twice, Peter scored once, and it brought the scores level at 7-7.

"How long are we playing this game for?" asked Clem.

"For as long as we want. It's unlimited time, so we can play all night, if we want to!" replied Alf.

"I'm not sure I want to play this all night, to be honest," stated Clem.

"I know, *I was only joking*!" exclaimed Alf.

The game ebbed and flowed, and the four players were beginning to cancel each other out, and nullifying the attacking play.

"What else is there to do?" asked Alf.

"Chat up the WRAFS!" exclaimed Clem. "There's enough of them about!"

"They'll have you for tea!" replied Alf.

"Maybe so. *But what a way to go*!" answered Clem.

"Yes, it has crossed my mind too!" joked Alf.

"Shall we play next goal wins?" proposed Clem.

"Yes, okay," agreed Alf, Peter and Gordon, in unison.

Five seconds later, Clem hit a crossfield shot from the wing, and it flew into the goal, to give Clem and Alf an 8-7 victory.

"Well played guys, you gave us a good game!" stated Alf with sincerity, and shaking both Peter "Squeaky" Bird and Gordon Gin Bottle by the hand. Clem followed suit, and was chuffed, but surprised, in the way he and Alf had come back from the brink of disaster, after trailing 6-2 at one stage. But football had an habit of springing shocks and surprises on the field, and it was no different with the table football pitch.

"We'll get our revenge at a later date, I'm sure!" replied Peter "Squeaky" Bird, who appeared disappointed with the result. He was still shaking his head in disbelief five minutes after the winning goal had been scored, and he couldn't believe he had ended up on the losing side.

"Yep, same teams for a re-match this time tomorrow, and we'll give your side another whupping!" joked Clem, with tongue in cheek.

"*That will be worth seeing*!" remarked Alf facetiously.

The four airmen stepped forward to the bar, and swiftly ordered their booze. Clem opted for a Coca Cola drink, as he was still only seventeen years of age, and not legally allowed to consume alcohol. The others were able to drink beer and spirits, as they had all reached the age of eighteen, and they slapped their thirsty lips together, in keen anticipation.

Clem looked around the NAAFI bar, and could not help but notice a bevy of beautiful women dancing in the middle of the room, on a shiny wooden dance floor, jigging, writhing, and getting down to the funky music. There were about twelve of them, and they were all letting their hair down, and moving to the groovy tunes. Clem was impressed with his first taste of the Women's Royal Air Force trainees, in the RAF Hereford NAAFI bar. The women had made a great effort to look good, with immaculate make-up applied to their features, including eye shadow and mascara, enhancing their already beautiful faces, and their hair was left long and dangling in a very sexy manner. These women were very attractive, and Clem could sense that these females who were having the fun, already knew how attractive they were, and they teased the boys relentlessly.

It was thirsty work for Clem and the others in his group, watching the WRAF'S dancing and cavorting, and the booze flowed well, as the guys sunk pint after pint of their respective drinks, in the hot sultry atmosphere of the disco room. Clem couldn't help but notice that these women were all dancing among themselves, even though there were an even number of men in the room. The guys had not found the nerve to ask any of the women to dance. Clem was wondering why these women had not obtained any male partners, and as he seemed to be the only sober one in his group, he realised why. The men were more interested in the beer, and getting drunk, then having a boogie with the beautiful women on the dance floor. It was *all a game.*

An hour or so later, when even more beer had been consumed, some of the males found the nerve to ask the gyrating women for a dance, and were promptly turned down. It was funny to watch, as the women were enjoying themselves so much, on their own. They did not want the company of any men, at that moment in time.

"Well, *aren't you going to chat up these WRAF's then, Clem?*" asked Alf, sinking his third pint of lager of the evening.

"Nope, I don't think I'll bother. These women are far too busy to chat. Look, they're all busy dancing!" replied Clem.

"Fair enough. There's plenty of fish in the sea!" answered Alf.

Clem was right. There was a time and a place to talk and get to know a woman, and at this present moment in time, this wasn't the right place. There would be other opportunities, Clem was sure. But he wasn't going to panic, and he wasn't all that desperate.

The slow dances began to play, and Clem stayed put. He watched with intrigue at the advances of some of the men, and they all struck lucky. The women who had earlier partied away on their own, were open to having a smooch and a cuddle with a complete stranger, and in some cases a snog, as the music slowed right down, with tracks such as "Love and Affection," by Joan Armatrading playing loudly and proudly, putting the couples in seventh heaven, for a short while.

Clem looked around for Alf, Peter and Gordon, to see where they had got to, and he was amazed to find them all on the dance floor, each with a WRAF, canoodling, groping and slow dancing to the next song, a Chicago track, "If You Leave Me Now." Clem was pleased for them, but didn't feel jealous. He wasn't ready to fuel his brain with lager, to give him the edge, when it came to finding the nerve, to ask a woman for a dance. That would come one day, sooner or later. For now, it was all about the learning curve of romance, drinking Coca Cola, and enjoying his music, in the smoky atmosphere of the NAAFI bar and disco.

When the music stopped and the lights went back on, the dance floor was quickly emptied by the loving couples. Clem looked around for his three mates, but there was no sign of any of them, they had all copped off, and were walking their women back separately, to the female accommodation block. Clem realised this, finished his drink, and made his way back to his billet room, *on his own*.

Clem woke up next day, after a decent night's sleep, and was keen to get up early, wash and dress and make his way to the Airmen's Mess for breakfast, sharpish, as he was starving. He glanced at his wristwatch, and discovered it was a quarter to seven. Not bad, considering if he had been at RAF Swinderby, he would have been woken up half an hour ago, by the sound of the reveille.

After shaving, freshening up and getting dressed into his RAF uniform, consisting of blue trousers, blue shirt, black tie, black shoes, black socks and blue woollen pullover, Clem looked around for some company, but everybody was still snoozing. It appeared to Clem that the hangovers from last night's booze fuelled session in the NAAFI had affected everyone, except him, the Coca Cola boy.

"Come on guys, it's time to get up! You know what Corporal McCauley's like, if you turn up late!" shouted Clem loudly, trying to rouse the slumbering trainees.

"Leave off!" yelled Alf King rudely, in reply, and he turned over to go back to sleep.

"Oi, don't be ridiculous, it's ten to seven. You need to get up!" called Clem, before grabbing his jacket and heading for the Airman's Mess.

Clem enjoyed his bacon, sausages, eggs, fried bread and beans with his bromide-free cup of tea, followed by two slices of toasted white bread, with relish. He looked around the room for his associates from the billet, but there was no sign of anyone. He decided to carry on and enjoy his breakfast, and he slurped keenly on his tea, chewed on his sausages and bacon, and enjoyed every morsel.

Eventually, one by one, his colleagues from the supply trade training course arrived at the Airmen's Mess, walking gingerly into the building, with their hands holding their aching heads. Alf King, Gordon Bottle and Peter Bird were the first three to arrive, and they chose their food carefully. They didn't look well at all. When they had settled down in their seats on Clem's table, to tuck into their food, Clem was quick to console them.

"How are you feeling lads?" asked Clem with empathy. "All okay?"

"No comment," replied Alf.

"I'll let you know after this," said Peter.

"*I'm not that bad*!" lied Gordon.

Clem chuckled at that last remark, because he could tell, not only by Gordon's blood shot eyes, but they looked like pee holes in the snow.

"That's cool! I'm sure you'll all feel a lot better, after a good plateful of a full English breakfast!" exclaimed Clem, with tongue in cheek.

At that, a couple of seconds later, Gordon Bottle dashed out of his chair, and headed straight for the Men's toilets, with both of his hands covering his mouth, to spare his blushes.

"Where's he off to?" asked Alf King.

"I dunno, *but he didn't look too well*," replied Clem facetiously.

"I think it was when you mentioned something about *the full English breakfast!*" exclaimed Alf.

At that, three seconds later, Peter Bird raced to the toilets, with his hands over his mouth, in exactly the same way.

"*I don't know! What can you say about these young un's today, not able to take their drink? Tut tut!*" commented Alf.

"I know, but all I said was full English breakfast, *that's no big deal*!" exclaimed Clem, with tongue in cheek.

At that, Alf King got up out of his chair, and with his face as white as a sheet, he too headed quickly for the Gents toilets, with both of his hands covering his mouth. Clem stared in disbelief. He could hardly believe what he was seeing. He looked down at the table where they had been sitting, and noticed the food on their plates had not been touched. At least they hadn't wasted any food, thought Clem. This can be warmed up for a later meal. He shook his head in amazement, then continued with his own breakfast, and slurped thirstily on his cup of tea.

Ten minutes later, the three ill blokes returned to the breakfast table, looking slightly better, as the colour had returned to their faces. But none of them was tempted to empty their plates of food. They decided to give it a very wide berth, for now.

Clem was lost for words to say. He had only ever been drunk once, when he went on a night out to a club, with his elder brother, in Hull city centre, at the Bierkeller, and had knocked back four bottles of Newcastle Brown Ale. He remembered vividly, when he got back home, that the room was spinning around and around, as he lay down in his bed. But thankfully, he wasn't sick. So that was a big consolation, and since then he hadn't touched a single drop of alcohol. And at seventeen years old, he knew it was illegal anyway. So it was a blessing in disguise that he had found out about the evils of alcohol, before he reached the legal age of eighteen.

"Aren't you having a cup of tea, or a coffee?" asked Clem, in a caring manner.

"Nope, I aint having anything," replied Alf.

"Nor me," seconded Peter.

"I'll not comment, thank you very much, as I'm trying to forget that food and drink exists, at this present moment in time," stated Gordon.

"Well, I hate to put this to you lads, but don't you think it's time we made a move to the Training Centre?" asked Clem.

The three hungover airmen all nodded together at the same time, in agreement. But they were careful on how keenly they nodded their heads, because even the smallest movement, hurt so much. Then they all took a steady stroll to the Training Centre.

"How many pints did you knock back, last night?" asked Clem.

"Six, I think. I lost count after that," replied Alf.

"Lightweight! I sunk eight, at least!" piped up Gordon proudly.

"Eleven, I think," answered Peter.

"Wow! *That's some going*!" exclaimed Clem.

"Tell me about it!" replied Peter.

"*Did you all pull*?" asked Clem, in mischief.

"Yep, I did. She was a red-headed Welsh lass," replied Alf.

"I pulled a brown haired, Scottish gal from Glasgow, and I couldn't understand a word she said! But she was fit though," revealed Gordon.

"I think I did, because I can't remember anything after leaving the dance floor. It was all a blur!" exclaimed Peter, with tongue in cheek.

"Oh dear! That's not good! So you don't know whether you walked a woman back to the WRAF's accomodation block, or not?" asked Clem, shaking his head.

"Yep, something like that," replied Peter. "As soon as the fresh air hit me, I was like a zombie," he explained.

"Been there, done that!" consoled Alf. "But not last night thankfully, *and last night was very memorable, to say the least*," he added.

"Oh yeah, how do you mean?" asked Clem, with intrigue.

"Never you mind. On second thoughts, *use your imagination*," replied Alf teasingly.

"You're taking the mickey, mate!" stated Clem, refusing to believe Alf's story.

"Whatever, please yourself. Oh sorry, that's what she said to me last night!" chuckled Alf.

"Are you seeing her again?" asked Clem.

"I'm not sure, maybe. I'll see how the land lies, between now and the end of the training course," replied Alf.

"What do you mean?" asked Clem.

"In other words, *there's plenty of fish in the sea*!" stated Alf.

"You're being quiet, Gordon. How was your time with the wee Scottish lassie?" asked Clem, with tongue in cheek.

"That's for me to know, and for you to never find out!" replied Gordon.

"That sounds worrying!" stated Alf.

"Why?" asked Gordon.

"Because you're being coy," replied Alf.

"So what! *that's my prerogative*," chuckled Gordon.

"It sounds like love!" exclaimed Peter.

"Love at first sight!" stated Alf.

"Maybe, *or maybe not*!" replied Gordon defensively.

"Give over, it sounds like a definite maybe to me!" stated Alf.

"Watch this space," replied Gordon.

"How about you Clem, *did you cop off at all*?" asked Peter.

"Nope, I was slow off the mark, and by the time I realised what was happening, it was too late, the WRAF's had all been snapped up!" replied Clem.

"Hard luck mate, but make sure you're on the ball next time," advised Alf, piping up again.

"Nah! *It's all a game*! I was watching the WRAF's dancing on their own for the majority of the evening, and then when it came to the slow dancing, the women were all over the blokes like a rash, for the sake of saving face, in front of their friends, as none of them wanted to be the odd one out!" stated Clem.

"That's very philosophical of you to notice, Clem," replied Alf.

"Yes, well, I did study Sociology at school and got an A, in the GCE O Level, last year, so I suppose some of that subject has rubbed off on me. It's my social sciences subconscious, coming to the fore, I suppose!" exclaimed Clem.

"Wow, A Level Sociology!" stated Alf.

"*No, not A Level*! Grade A, in O Level, *to be precise*," replied Clem.

"Well, that's the same thing in my book. It's still a grade A! Well done! But with grades like that, don't you think you're over qualified to be an RAF Supplier?" asked Alf.

"Yes, maybe I am, or maybe I'm not," replied Clem.

"Well, at least you can use your grade A Sociology O Level to good effect, in the RAF. That's officer material!" exclaimed Alf.

"*Oh, I don't know about that*. But Sociology has definitely helped me when it comes to the mystery of what makes a woman tick, that's for sure!" exclaimed Clem.

"*Perhaps you should write a book about it*?" suggested Alf.

"Ha, that sounds like a very good idea," agreed Clem.

"It could sell a million, if it explains what makes a woman tick!" joked Alf, with tongue in cheek.

"I shall start writing it as soon as I can!" replied Clem, continuing with the jokey conversation.

"*Because I haven't the foggiest idea, what makes a woman tick*," admitted Alf.

"Buy the book then, and learn!" joked Clem.

"Don't worry about that, I'll be the first to buy a copy, that's for sure!" replied Alf.

The four airmen stopped at the front door of the RAF Hereford Supply Training Headquarters, and they all took a deep breath of fresh air, before letting themselves into the stuffy classroom. It was five minutes to nine. They had arrived a few minutes early, which made a welcome change, and they promptly headed inside the room. They were all shocked to discover that the rest of the trainees had already arrived, and were waiting patiently for Clem, Alf, Peter and Gordon to get there, before they could begin the second day of trade training.

"Come on in chaps, come on in!" shouted Corporal McCauley amicably.
Clem, Alf, Gordon and Peter scuttled into the classroom, as quickly as possible, and felt as guilty as sin. Even though they were five minutes early, arriving last had made them feel awful. They all found a seat, which conveniently, was the same one as yesterday.
"Don't panic lads, you're not late, so don't look so worried!" exclaimed Corporal McCauley, with empathy in his tone.

Clem smiled wryly, and both Alf and Gordon nodded in acknowledgement, whilst Peter didn't say or do anything. His head was all over the place, after last night's drinking session.

 "So, welcome to Day Two of the Royal Air Force Hereford supply trade training course. I hope you are all well, and had a good night's sleep. These mornings come around quickly, don't they? Which is why I always try to cram in as much as I can, into the waking hours, because you waste a hell of a lot time sleeping!" stated Corporal McCauley.

Alf, Gordon and Peter knew exactly what Corporal McCauley was talking about, but they didn't care. They all felt as rough as the bottom of a budgie's bird cage, and all they needed right now was sleep, and lots of it, to recover from the copious amounts of booze they had knocked back in the NAAFI bar last night.

Nobody else seemed affected. Clem was feeling fine, and the two Scots, Daniel MacJames and Luke Jappy were either very good actors, hiding their hangovers, or they hadn't touched a drop of alcohol the previous night. It was more likely to be the former, rather than the latter, as they both loved a good drink, which was Scotch whisky. The rest of the airmen all appeared in fine fettle too, so it seemed it was only Alf King, Gordon Bottle and Peter Bird, that felt like death warmed up.

The three of them had plans to do as little thinking as possible, and hoped that Corporal McCauley didn't bother them with any trivial questions, because the trio knew they could not cope with any of that today.

 "Is anybody suffering from a hangover this morning?" asked Corporal McCauley, in a somewhat softer, quieter voice than normal.

"No corporal!" replied eleven trainees in unison. The other three, Alf King, Gordon Bottle and Peter Bird remained silent. They could not lie. They hoped Corporal McCauley didn't notice. How wrong were they? He noticed everything, but he didn't let on to the fact immediately.

"Good, so everyone is as sober as a judge, then?" stated Corporal McCauley in a very loud, booming voice, which rang in the ears of the three hungover airmen, Alf, Gordon and Peter, and rattled their aching heads, making them feel ten times worse.

"Yes corporal!" bellowed the eleven airmen, together in unison again, for the second time.

Corporal McCauley nodded in acknowledgement.

"Good! Good!" he barked loudly.

Alf, Gordon and Peter held their sensitive heads in their hands, and wished break time would hurry up, so they could swill a bucket load of tea and coffee down their throats. But the seconds seemed like hours and the minutes seemed like days. It was no good, this hangover was ruining their lives.

"Now, the Supply Squadron, as you all realise after yesterday's training, has a Voucher System. This Voucher System is tried and tested and is the best we have at this present moment in time. I'm sure it will go from strength to strength and be fully incorporated within the computer network of the Royal Air Force, in due course," began Corporal McCauley. "At the moment, only SCAAF supply the Vouchers by computer, but I'm sure the Clothing Store, Technical Store, Electronic Stores Group, Petrol Oils and Lubricants and Receipt and Despatch will all be equipped in the very near future, with a computer, to enable them to function more efficiently, without waiting for SCAAF to issue the Vouchers," added Corporal McCauley, speaking loudly, clearly and enthusiastically, which continued to rattle inside the delicate heads of Alf King, Gordon Bottle and Peter Bird, who were all keenly clock watching. But the minutes continued to tick by, slower than ever.

"What does SCAAF stand for, *Alf King*?" called Corporal McCauley.

"Erm, Supply Account Control Flight!" replied Alf quickly, in a blind panic, and without any thought given to his answer.

"Nope, wrong!" said Corporal McCauley.

"Huh, sorry. I meant Supply Control And Accounting Flight," corrected Alf, instantly.

"Yep, that's better. You got your words mixed up a bit there, so be careful in the future. It's SCAAF not SACF. Any more answers like that one, and you shall be sacked!" joked Corporal McCauley facetiously. He cleared his throat, took a long swig of water from his cup, and paused for a short time, to collect his thoughts. "How many copies are there of the Voucher, *Gordon Bottle*?" asked Corporal McCauley.

"Three, corporal," replied Gordon, after scratching his head, and working it out slowly.

"Correct, that's good," stated Corporal McCauley. "Now of those three copies, please tell me where they are issued, *Peter Bird*," added the corporal.

"SCAAF, *for one*," stuttered Peter. "Erm, to the department that ordered the goods, *for two*, and a copy is kept by the issuer, *for three*," replied Peter gingerly, speaking with great care and caution, as he nursed his aching, banging head, that throbbed with every word spoken.

"Yes, you're right in a way, but they're not technically in the correct order. *Copy One* is sent to SCAAF, *Copy Two* is retained by the Supplier and *Copy Three* is despatched with the goods. Does everyone follow that okay? *Peter Bird*?" asked Corporal McCauley.

"Yes corporal," replied Peter.

"Yes corporal," answered the rest of the trainees together, in unison.

"Okay, and on that note, it's time you all took a well earned break! Be back here in fifteen minutes," ordered Corporal McCauley.

The fourteen airmen rose to their feet to leave the room, and were quickly on their way to the vending machine, for a welcome cuppa. No more so than the three hungover airmen, Alf, Gordon and Peter.

"I could sink a barrel of tea!" exclaimed Alf, as he left the room.

"Me too, my head feels like it's been kicked around Wembley stadium!" agreed Gordon.

"Anyone got any painkillers? As all the tea in the world won't take away my headache! It's a killer, and easily the worse headache I've ever had in my life!" piped up Peter.

There was no reply to that question from any of the trainees. Everyone shook their heads and Peter feared the worst.

"Does that mean I've got to ask Corporal McCauley, for some painkillers?" groaned Peter.

"Nope, not really. The NAAFI shop should sell them. Why don't you go and pop there to buy a packet? It won't take you five minutes," suggested Clem.

"I can't be bothered walking up there. It's way too far, and if I'm late back, Corporal McCauley will go nuts, and might throw me off the course! No, I think I'll grin and bear it," replied Peter, putting on a brave face.

"Are you sure?" asked Clem.

"Yes, I'm positive. I'll buy some at lunch, when I've got more time to myself. I'm not risking my career, for the sake of an headache," replied Peter.

"Okay, fair enough," said Clem.

"What's up Peter?" asked Gordon.

"I need some painkillers," replied Peter.

"Ask Corporal McCauley," suggested Gordon.

"No, *I'm not letting him know I'm hungover*," replied Peter. "He'll kick me off the course."

"*I know! Why don't we all ask Corporal McCauley for painkillers*? That way we cover ourselves. He can't kick everyone off the course. He'll think it's an epidemic, or something!" stated Clem shrewdly.

"Good idea! Strength in numbers!" replied Gordon.

Clem called for all the trainees to congregate in a huddle, in the corner of the refreshments room, beside the vending machine.

"Listen in guys. We're on a mission to save Peter "Squeaky" Bird from the chop! He's suffering from the worst ever hangover, after sinking eleven pints last night. But he's afraid of asking for painkillers, just in case Corporal McCauley kicks him off the course. So, what I've come up with, is a plan to save his RAF career, and cure his hangover at the same time! What I suggest is, when Peter asks Corporal McCauley for a couple of painkillers, for his headache, we all pipe up and ask for some too. That way, it'll cover Peter, as the corporal won't be able to kick us all off the course! Is everybody with me on this?" asked Clem in a hushed, whispered voice.

"Yep," replied the other twelve trainees in unison, nodding in approval.

"Great! Thanks chaps!" said Clem, with a wide, beaming smile.

The trainees trooped into the classroom, without having been called in by the corporal. Peter Bird was feeling worse by the second, whilst Gordon Bottle and Alf King seemed better, after the tea they had consumed.

Clem looked across at Peter Bird, and he could see how ill he was. His face was pale white, his eyes were bloodshot, and his whole body language cried out, "severely hungover!" But the request for painkillers from Peter did not materialise. Clem wondered why. He had announced it to the other trainees, but it looked like Peter had chickened out, and had decided he could wait until lunch time. Clem decided to do nothing, and then without warning, just as Corporal McCauley was preparing to hand out some reading material, Peter "Squeaky" Bird raised his hand.

"Excuse me corporal, but may I have some painkillers please, as I'm not feeling too well," stated Peter.

Corporal McCauley stared at the stricken airmen for a short while, and didn't say a word, before nodding and smiling.

"Of course, the medicine cabinet is in that cupboard over there!" replied Corporal McCauley, pointing to the corner of the room.

"Is it okay if I have some painkillers too, corporal?" asked Clem.

"Yeah sure, follow Peter," replied Corporal McCauley.

"And me, as well, because I feel dreadful," piped up Alf King.

"So do I, can I have some?" asked Gordon Bottle.

Corporal McCauley looked on at the trainees in amazement.

"Hang on! Hang on! What's going on here? *You cannot all be ill!*" exclaimed Corporal McCauley, with suspicion in his tone.

"*I am*!" replied Peter "Squeaky" Bird, with determination.

"*So am I!*" stated Alf.

"*And me*!" said Gordon.

"Look, I'm not having this!" yelled Corporal McCauley. Clem stepped backwards, and tried to hide into the background, but was spotted by Corporal McCauley. Peter managed to swallow the two painkilling tablets, with the help of a cup of tea he had brought with him, from the vending machine outside.

"Is there anybody else feeling ill?" asked Corporal McCauley.

The whole of the trainees in the classroom, raised their hand.

"What! All of you?" shrieked Corporal McCauley. "You're taking the Mickey!" he bawled.

"Yes corporal!" bellowed the trainees together, in unison.

"Well, if that's the case, you'd better have some painkillers. But I'm not happy. If this continues, I may have to send you all to the Medical Centre, for a check up!" replied Corporal McCauley.

Clem gasped with a sigh of relief, at his successful plan bearing fruit, as he returned to his chair.

"*What about you, Clem?*" asked Corporal McCauley.

"I'll be okay, thanks corporal," replied Clem, now feeling a little guilty after pulling a fast one.

"Are you sure?" asked Corporal McCauley.

"Yep, I'll be fine," reiterated Clem.

Corporal McCauley shook his head in amazement, at Clem's miraculous recovery.

"Okay, now if any of you worsen as the day wears on, please let me know, and I'll whisk you quickly off to the Medical Centre," informed Corporal McCauley.

"Yes corporal!" replied the trainees, in unison.

Clem couldn't help but grin with relief, at helping out a mate in need, and Peter perked up rapidly, after consuming the two strong painkillers.

The trainees listened keenly, and Corporal McCauley taught with skill, patience, endeavour, diligence and commitment. His Irish accent was becoming stronger as the day wore on, and that was because he was feeling less under pressure as a teacher and coach, and the happier he became, the more relaxed he was, and this brought out his strong Irish twang, to the fore. He'd had a very long day already, having risen at 4am for a road run, to keep his momentum going for the next marathon he intended to compete in, for the Royal Air Force. But he was on the ball today.

"Now, next on the training agenda guys is the familiarisation of the Voucher, and knowing what is what, in each of the panels. As you all know, each copy is a duplicate of the number One copy, so it's the same all the way through. There's no hidden catches, and no tricks designed to trip you up," began Corporal McCauley.

He wandered over to his cup of water again, and helped himself to another long, refreshing gulp, to quench his raging thirst. He liked to keep his throat hydrated and moist, and there wasn't anything better than a cup of still, cold water.

"If you take a look at the example of the Voucher, I have just handed out to you all, please check the panel marked "Description." This is where you'll find the subject matter, otherwise known as the goods or the parts. So, for example, it could read, say, for arguments sake, a hammer, or a hacksaw, or a chisel. You'll find the title of the goods in this location," explained Corporal McCauley. "Next is quantity, and please read this carefully, as it could be a matter of life or death, because if an engineering squadron are in need of twelve altimeters, please send twelve, as it may be working on twelve aircrafts, all at the same time, preparing for a tactical sortie. So, if you send one or two, that will hold up the other ten or eleven aircrafts from flying, and in the process, stopping vital training time for the pilots and navigators. So, please, please, please read the quantity box carefully!" exclaimed Corporal McCauley, with a straight face. "This all sounds simple and easy, now, here in the classroom. But, I can assure you, it isn't as straightforward as you may think. When you're under pressure, you are likely to make mistakes. But, what I need to make clear to you all, is this. When you are under pressure with the workload, and the intensity of the job is getting to you, please remember back to this training room, and what I advised you to do. Double check the number in the Quantity Box, as this is the most important item printed on the Voucher. The quantity that is ordered needs to be spot on at all times, so read it once, and check it twice, and do it right, first time!" advised Corporal McCauley loudly, keenly and slowly.

"Yes corporal!" replied the trainees in unison, and together as one.

"The next box to look out for, is the location, which is also a matter of life or death, as haste and speed is the order of the day! The sooner you locate the item, the better. As the goods can be despatched efficiently and delivered on time, and in turn, have the aircraft flying high, as soon as possible! We are here to help keep those planes in the air!" exclaimed Corporal McCauley.

"Yes corporal!" piped up the trainees, in agreement.

"Now, the Voucher is a valuable piece of property, and is to be respected at all times! No defacing is allowed, including cutting, shredding, marking with a pen, nor crumpling. This is a valid piece of Royal Air Force equipment, that is crucial in the role of the modern fighting force. Under no circumstances whatsoever, will you be allowed to change anything on the Voucher, by means of a writing implement, including a biro pen, pencil or a marker pen. All the information on the Voucher is programmed into the system, which tallies the quantity and description together, and nobody, *and I mean nobody*, whoever they may be, *is allowed to tamper with the info displayed.* It is a Court Martial offence for anybody seen to be meddling with the Royal Air Force Supply Squadron's Vouchers! Is that understood?" demanded Corporal McCauley.

"Yes corporal!" replied the fourteen trainees, together in unison.

"Good. As long as you know, you won't fall into the trap. If there is a shortage at the location point, when you are picking the goods, let your superior officer, or NCO know about it, as soon as possible," stated Corporal McCauley.

"Will do, corporal!" called the trainees, in acknowledgement.

"The normal ranking system of AC, LAC, SAC, Corporal, Sergeant and Flight Sergeant is commonly found in the Royal Air Force, and it is no different in the Supply Squadron. Usually a newbie from here at RAF Hereford is posted to an RAF station and is then taken under the wing of a Senior Aircraftman or Senior Aircraftwoman, aka SAC or SACW, to provide valuable assistance to the newbie, and being their reliable training buddy. As you will all find out, *once you leave here, the real work begins,* and you'll be forever learning. The training is everlasting! Now, the Technical Store for instance has a scenario such as this, with a Corporal, Sergeant and a Flight Sergeant running the show, and with the Flight Lieutenant overseeing the whole shebang. You will hardly ever see the Flight Lieutenant to be honest, except if you are deployed on Petrol Oils and Lubricants, where the Flight Lieutenant is present to perform weekly dips of the aviation fuel tanks, on a designated day," informed Corporal McCauley, pausing to pour himself another refreshing cup of ice cold water, from the jug on his table.

"Your present role requirements as an AC, also known as an Aircraftman, is to listen, learn and work as hard as you can, to reach your next ranking, which is Leading Aircraftman, that you will earn on successful completion of this training course. And after this, you will need to continue with your progress, to obtain promotion to Senior Aircraftman, and from there the world's your oyster! A lot of airmen and airwomen are happy to plod on in the RAF, as SAC's or SACW's, but some are keen to attain the next rung of the promotion ladder, which is Corporal. *It's up to you what you do*, but I'm positive you'll find life in the Royal Air Force very rewarding, if you rise up through the ranks, which includes an increase in pay, too, but that's academic, at this stage. It's only when you own a house, get married and have children, that you will see the importance of higher wages!" stated Corporal McCauley facetiously, and with tongue in cheek.

Clem thought deeply about the ranking system, and he was determined to make sure that he put everything into his efforts, to make a success of his time in the Royal Air Force, and to try and enjoy every working day.

Corporal McCauley was continuing to keep an eye on all the trainees, that were present in the classroom, after they had complained of feeling unwell earlier, and he had to admit to himself that he was still worried about Gordon Bottle, Alf King and Peter Bird. He decided the best course of action was to open a few windows, even though it was late November, the temperatures outside were not all that bad. After swinging open two or three panels of glass, he was quite satisfied that he had let some welcome RAF Hereford fresh air into the room. He continued to watch Bottle, King and Bird, in particular, who seemed to be looking the worst of the trio, and he wasn't sure if Clem Harrison was okay either. But he made sure he monitored him too, along with the other trainees, as he didn't want to lose any of them on the second day.

"Okay, okay trainees! *So, everyone's feeling well?*" asked Corporal McCauley, clapping his hands together, to get attention.

"Yes corporal!" yelled the trainees keenly, in reply.

"Very good! Don't forget to let me know if you're start feeling ill again," stated Corporal McCauley diligently.

"Yes corporal!" reiterated the trainees.

"Let's continue then, with the training course," began Corporal McCauley, grabbing another swig of water from the cup on his desk. He could see that it needed a refill, and he helped himself to more water from the large jug sitting on the window sill.

"I'm talking about Receipt and Despatch in this session, which is an integral part of the Supply Squadron, that helps keep the Royal Air Force machine ticking over. You may be deployed in R and D, which is short for Receipt and Despatch, and let me tell you, it's a job that requires numerical skills, dexterity, a positive mental attitude and diligence, to name a few. Working in R and D, is rewarding and hectic, but it' s a lot of fun, for the right person, with the proper attitude. And you will never be bored working in there, as there's alway something happening," stated Corporal McCauley confidently.

Clem nodded in acknowledgement, and it crossed his mind that it might be a good place to work, if he didn't happen to slot into a position in Petrol Oils and Lubricants, as he had hoped. It was food for thought, and another option for him to consider.

"In R and D, you shall pack, unpack, stock take, check items against the Voucher, and keep everything tickety-boo, with an upbeat attitude, and still have time to sweep up the floor, at the end of the day, thus keeping the bay clean and tidy. It's no job for shiny arses!" exclaimed Corporal McCauley.

Clem and the rest of the trainees in the classroom laughed at that quip, as it was the first time any of them had heard it before. But they need not have bothered to ask what it meant, as it explained itself.

"There's early mornings and late finishes, because it all depends on the wagons rolling in, and out. There is an Early Bird delivery from RAF Stafford, which is the centralised depot for goods being despatched. Everything goes through RAF Stafford. It's the hub of the Supply Squadron, in the Royal Air Force, *and some of you may be posted there*, whether you've placed it in your three choices for posting, or not. It depends on how busy RAF Stafford are, and if they're short staffed. *You'll love RAF Stafford*!" exclaimed Corporal McCauley sarcastically, with tongue in cheek. He paused for another refreshing drink of water, and caught his breath.

"I'm sure you're all hungry, and could eat a horse for lunch!" the corporal exclaimed. "Well, I've some good news, it's time for something to eat. But don't go there expecting to eat Red Rum, or you'll have me to answer to!" joked Corporal McCauley. "Be back here in an hour, please!"

Clem and the rest of the trainees got up from their chairs and made a beeline for the Airman's Mess. Clem checked his watch for the time, and noticed it was a couple of minutes to twelve midday. The morning had soon passed, he thought.

The airmen queued up for lunch, and Clem noticed some WRAF's were waiting ahead of him. There were a few nice looking ones, that took Clem's eye, and one of those turned her head to look at Clem, and she smiled. Clem returned the smile, and she giggled in reply. Clem stepped back to take a closer look at her, and he could not help but notice her lovely long legs, that were very shapely, wrapped up in a pair of black WRAF tights, underneath a baggy blue WRAF skirt. Clem liked what he saw, and was impressed. The WRAF turned towards the food counter, and was away into the distance, moving among the crowd. All Clem could see was her red hair, cut in a bob style, moving forwards.

Clem gathered up his plates of food on a tray, and went to find a place to sit down. The Airmen's Mess was extremely busy, and there was hardly anywhere to breathe, never mind eat lunch. He decided to plonk himself down on a table, where there was a solitary spare place, and he sat among a group of strangers.

"Hey up buddy! How are you doing?" piped up one of the airmen, a confident, brown haired chap, in his early twenties, that was sat opposite.

"Not bad, thanks! What about yourself?" replied Clem.

"I'm doing fine! Where are you from, buddy?" asked the airman cheekily.

"I'm from Hull, what about you?" replied Clem, tucking into his plateful of food.

"Hull? Are you really? Wow, me too!" gasped the airman in shock.

"It's a small world!" exclaimed Clem.

"It sure is! What trade are you?" asked the friendly airman.

"Supply, what about you?" replied Clem.

"Steward," answered the friendly airman. "My name's Brad, by the way!"

"Pleased to meet you Brad, my name's Clem."

"So, how did you travel here?" asked Brad.

"By train, what about you?" replied Clem.

"Car, it's a lot quicker. I can cut the journey time in half!" answered Brad.

"Wow, can you? That's great!" exclaimed Clem.

"How long did it take you to travel here, by train?" asked Brad.

"About eight hours or so, altogether, I think," replied Clem.

"Yeah, well, you see. It took me only four hours to get here in my car, and I reckon it'll take me the same to get back, on Friday night!" exclaimed Brad.

"Not bad!" replied Clem.

"Yep, it's a no brainer!" answered Brad.

"Good, good," enthused Clem, continuing to fill his face with his food.

"As for the journey by car. It's a piece of piss!" reiterated Brad with a smirk.

"Okay," replied Clem.

"*Do you want a lift back to Hull, at the weekend?*" asked Brad.

"No thanks, I'm staying here," replied Clem.

"Are you sure?" asked Brad.

"Yes, I'm positive. But thanks all the same!" replied Clem.

"Okay, but if you change your mind, let me know, okay buddy?" stated Brad.

"Yep, will do," agreed Clem, knowing full well he was happy staying at RAF Hereford at the weekend. He had only just got there, the day before yesterday, so he had no intention of travelling back all those miles, even if the journey time had been cut in half. Clem knew there was far more fun to be had at RAF Hereford, especially with a feast of eye candy to look at, in the shape of the attractive WRAFs, in their dozens.

Clem continued with his lunch, which consisted of pork, carrots, sprouts, mashed potato and gravy, followed closely by chocolate sponge and custard, and then eagerly washed down with tea, without bromide. It was delicious as usual, and ten times better than the food at RAF Swinderby, and it was close to being as good as his mother's cooking.

As he sat back after eating his lunch, his eyes roved around looking for the cute WRAF redhead from earlier, but she was nowhere to be seen. He shrugged his shoulders, sighed and looked forward to catching up with her later on.

With lunch over and done with, Clem got up from his chair and walked to the NAAFI newsagents to buy a paper. He needed to see what was going on in the outside world. Just like when he was at RAF Swinderby, the world could have ended for all Clem knew, with only the RAF stations left in operation. He had to see for himself, if this was true.

After buying his newspaper, he walked back to the billet and rested up on his bed. He need not have worried, as the world was still ticking over, as usual, but there wasn't any real great news to read. It was all straightforward and hunky dory, with life outside going through the motions, including the football clubs he was interested in, Aston Villa, Tottenham Hotspur and Hull City, and also Hull Kingston Rovers, on the rugby league front.

Clem discarded the newspaper on to his bedside cabinet, before jumping off his bed and making tracks to the Supply Squadron Training Centre. The lunch hour had gone too fast, and it was time to knuckle down again, and return to the nitty gritty once more. The weather had changed. It was now pouring down with rain.

When Clem got back to the Supply Squadron Training Centre, he was shocked to discover there was a depleted class of trainees, sitting in the classroom. There was no sign of Gordon Bottle, Alf King or Peter Bird, and a few others too. He wondered what had happened to them, and he waited with bated breath in his chair, at the place where he had been sitting all week.

Corporal McCauley was standing at the front of the classroom, and he was waiting until the clock on the wall struck one o'clock. It was currently five minutes to one. More trainees began to troop inside, including Luke Jappy, Daniel MacJames, Norman Shepherd, Gerry Joseph and Simon Roberts. But there was still no sign of Alf King, Peter Bird or Gordon Bottle.

Corporal McCauley waited another couple of minutes to let the trainees settle down in their places, before he prepared himself to speak. There was a lot of noise coming from the eleven airmen.

"Alright, alright guys! Hush yourself down, now!" yelled Corporal McCauley.

There was instant silence, as the airmen immediately obeyed the order from the NCO instructor.

"Now, as you can see. We are three men down this afternoon. AC King, AC Bottle and AC Bird. They've been whisked off to the Medical Centre for observation, after complaining about being struck down by a stomach bug. I feel it's more than that, but what do I know, I'm not a doctor. But at least they are in the best place to get the ideal treatment and hopefully they'll be back here, in next to no time, to catch up. So, without any further ado, we shall continue with the training course!" exclaimed Corporal McCauley.

Clem's mind boggled. He wondered about Alf, Gordon and Peter and whether they had been sussed out by Corporal McCauley, in respect of their hangover, or whether they had owned up, with a guilty conscience. It would all come out in the wash, reckoned Clem, sooner or later. And whether Alf, Gordon and Peter survived, only time would tell.

"Before we start, is there anybody else suffering from this mystery sickness bug?" asked Corporal McCauley.

"No corporal!" replied the trainees, together in unison.

"Are you sure?" asked Corporal McCauley.

"Yes corporal!" insisted the trainees.

"Okay, that's fine! Off we go again. Let's move on with the course. If you remember before lunch, we covered Receipt and Despatch. Now we shall go over the rudiments of SCAAF, otherwise known as Supply Control And Accounting Flight, and some of you may be deployed in this department. That's if your marks on this course are high enough, as you need to be bright to work in SCAAF!"

began Corporal McCauley, pausing to pour himself another chilled cup of water. "SCAAF is where it all happens. It's an office based job that controls the Vouchers, and is manned by extremely clever people, who can think on their bums. Yep, you've got it, they're shiny arses! *But intelligent shiny arses*!" exclaimed the corporal. "As I said before, this training course will determine whether you're good enough for SCAAF, or not. So pay attention, and you could strike it lucky!" he added.

Clem shook his head at the thought of working in SCAAF. It just wasn't his cup of tea. He couldn't see himself sitting down, working in an office, for all the tea in China. And Clem loved his tea! The thought of working in an enclosed environment filled him with dread, and fear. He knew he wouldn't be able to handle it in an office. He recalled the time he was working as a temporary office junior, at the Hull City Council, prior to joining the Royal Air Force, and how he hated being cooped up inside a claustrophobic space. He pledged however, not to halt his commitment to the RAF Hereford Supply Squad Trade Training, just for the sake of forfeiting his chance to work in SCAAF. Clem was still determined to continue working hard, studying as best he could, and doing as well as possible. It was in his best interests that he concentrated, and made the most of his opportunity in the Royal Air Force, as it had been an ambition of his to join up, ever since he had seen a demonstration of the RAF careers, at his high school, when he was 14 years old. He knew there and then that is what he wanted to do, so there was no way he would waste this chance, for the sake of avoiding working in SCAAF.

"Okay fine, that's SCAAF then. Now, the next department to briefly explain, is Petrol Oils and Lubricants. This is a complicated section within the Supply

Squadron and involves early and late shifts, depending when the aviation fuel tanks need refilling by the bulk fuel tankers from FINA, and when the bowsers on the airfield require replenishing to serve the aircraft. The early morning sorties require airmen and airwomen to be available to fill the bowsers, and this also applies to the late night sorties. Some start as early as seven o'clock in the morning, and some finish as late as eleven o'clock at night. An airman or airwoman deployed in this department known as POL for short, has to be on duty around the clock, meaning in essence, it is a twenty four hour job. Also, the RAF personnel vehicles need refuelling in out of working hours time, such as the RAF police for instance, or the RAF fire service, or the RAF air traffic control. It all depends on the nature of the duty of the services, within the RAF station that you are deployed at, but the Petrol Oils and Lubricants personnel have to be prepared to work unsociable hours. If that suits you, great! The job's for you! If not, then tough, you need to move away from this, as it ain't a normal nine till five position!" exclaimed Corporal McCauley.

Clem listened with interest. He wasn't bothered about working unsociable hours. In fact it was something he would relish, as he wasn't one for moaning about working too much, at any time of the day, whether it was morning, noon or night. If a job needed doing, he was prepared to do it well, at any hour. So night shifts, evening shifts and early morning shifts would be no problem to Clem. He always worked with a smile on his face.

"Petrol Oils and Lubricants is spread over a large area. There are refuelling sites out on the airfield, in the middle of nowhere. The Liquid Oxygen site is located at the other end of the airfield, well away from the office buildings and domestic quarters, and the cylinder storage unit is also situated outside, well away from the refuelling site and Liquid Oxygen compound. The storage units for the paints, oils and lubricants are also dispersed away from any of the other explosive products. So, as you can see, there is a wide area to cover and it shall keep you fit and active. It's great for the lover of the outdoors. But not so good if you can't bear the cold and wet. You'd be better off as a shiny arse in SCAAF!" bellowed Corporal McCauley, with tongue in cheek.

Clem didn't have to worry about being a shiny arse. There was no way on earth that was going to happen.

"Next on the agenda, is something the Royal Air Force has only just invested in. It's a brand new concept for the Supply Squadron, and the whole world in general. But when it takes off, I reckon it'll take over, and save a heck of a lot of paperwork. *What am I talking about?* Computers, of course. Has anyone worked on a computer before?" enquired Corporal McCauley.

"No, corporal!" replied the trainees.

"Well, that's alright then, you're all in the same boat," stated Corporal McCauley. "Now, the computer is a simple piece of kit, and there's nothing to worry about. It's a glorified typewriter, that happens to store information for future use, and can be saved on the hardware inside the computer, or on the software, which is a floppy disc. But whatever you use, please make sure the work is saved to one, or both. There's nothing worse than having to re-key the work twice. The computer is the future of the Royal Air Force, and SCAAF is the main user of this new concept, although the other departments within the Supply Squadron are awaiting delivery of their very own

Information Technology apparatus, as we speak," explained Corporal McCauley.

The afternoon passed quickly for Clem, as Corporal McCauley showed a film all about the Supply Squadron, and what it meant to the Royal Air Force. It explained everything a new starter needed to know, about working as a Supplier in the modern RAF. But this trade was the brunt of a million jokes, ranging from calling those employed in there, as a "storebasher," "stacker" and blanket stacker." But like everything in the Royal Air Force, all the trades had the Mickey taken out of them, in a humorous way, and it was nothing to be ashamed about. It was pure RAF banter. The film showed what everyday life was like in the Supply Squadron and Clem enjoyed it immensely, and before he knew it, it was time to pack up for the day.

Clem queued up for tea. He was famished. He fancied steak, chips and peas, and he hoped it was on the menu, this evening. He wasn't disappointed. As he got to the front of the long queue, he could see the solitary sizzling steak staring him in the face. It was a heart-warming and welcoming sight and had his name written all over it. He was chuffed to bits when he found that nobody else in front of him in the queue, had opted for it. He grabbed the steak quickly, and scattered a portion of chips next to it on the plate, and then instantly scooped a serving of peas, to finish off his main course.

In the corner of his eye, he could see the hot, red-headed female WRAF from earlier, and he gawped at her gormlessly. He was like a rabbit in headlights, and he stared open mouthed. She was stunning in Clem's estimation, and as he looked at her, he forgot how hot his dinner plate was, and when he picked it up to make room for his pudding, he burnt his fingers.

"You're not supposed to touch your dinner plate, mate! That's why it's on a tray!" exclaimed the duty chef, from across the dining room.

"Oops, silly me!" replied Clem, blushing a deep red, in embarrassment.

The gorgeous WRAF redhead glanced over at Clem and smiled, and Clem smiled back, totally forgetting his blistering fingers.

"It must be love!" yelled the same chef.

Clem didn't react and looked for a place to sit. It was full in the Airmen's Mess again, and he couldn't get anywhere near the hot redhead, so he sat down in the next available chair, at the other side of the building.

Clem intermittently glanced up at the redhead, to give her the eye, and she did the same. Then she got up and walked towards him, and he expected her to come over and sit down, but she mysteriously walked straight past, towards the exit. Her eyes had been fixed firmly on Clem, and Clem's eyes were permanently looking at her. But alas, the couple had still not interacted properly in a one-to-one conversation, and it was something Clem was ardently waiting for.

The RAF Hereford scran was delicious, and Clem sunk his cup of tea, to wash down all the grease from his chips and fried steak. He enjoyed his apple crumble and custard too. After he had put the final piece of pie into his mouth, which was smothered in custard, Clem was joined by the three stricken airmen, Alf King, Peter Bird and Gordon Bottle.

"Hey lads, how are you doing?" called Clem.

"Not bad, thanks!" replied Alf.

"Better than this morning!" stated Gordon.

"Bloody terrible!" revealed Peter, with honesty.

"What happened?" asked Clem.

"Don't ask!" shrieked Alf.

"Why, what's up?" asked Clem.

"Corporal McCauley rumbled us!" explained Gordon.

"What do you mean?" asked Clem, with a frown.

"He sussed us out, and we had to do the straight line test!" exclaimed Gordon.

"*Straight line test, what's that*?" asked Clem dumbly.

"It's when you make a mug of yourself, trying to walk a very narrow plank, in a straight line, and fall off!" piped up Peter Bird.

Clem had to stifle a laugh, as it sounded very funny, but he knew it would be rude and disrespectful to the three hungover airmen, that were looking worse for wear, so he decided to stay amicable.

"Oh okay, and did you pass?" asked Clem.

"Nope! If they had been sharks in the water, either side of the plank, we'd have all been eaten!" exclaimed Peter comically.

"Gulp!" replied Clem, feeling his stomach turn over. He was thankful he had finished his meal. "So what's happening with the training course, are you still on it?"

"Yep, just about! We've been given a warning to stay sober! If we are caught hungover again, we are off the course!" mumbled Alf quietly, not wanting to let any ears nearby, tune in to his revelation.

"Careful with the booze tonight, then lads," advised Clem.

"Don't worry, I'm tea total for the remainder of this course, that's for sure!" stated Alf wholeheartedly.

"Me too!" seconded Peter.

"And me!" called Gordon.

"Good for you!" replied Clem.

Clem let the three tuck into their evening meal, as he could see they were hungry, and they ate like starving gannets. They had all chosen a greasy meal of bacon, eggs, sausages and fried tomatoes, and had not let up on the quantity, as each of the three plates were filled to the edge. Clem chuckled to himself, as he recalled how Peter had described walking the plank, and how they had failed to cross it successfully. It was the way he had said it.

"What's it going to be tonight, then lads, NAAFI again?" asked Clem brightly.

"You've got to be joking, mate!" replied Gordon abruptly.

"Nope, I'm off to the land of nod!" stated Alf.

"I might well give it a go, Clem. The hair of the dog that bit you, and all that!" exclaimed Peter.

"You mug!" joked Alf, with tongue in cheek.

"Yep, you're asking for trouble, if you're going to get bladdered again!" remarked Gordon.

"Nope, don't worry. I'm not touching a drop of alcohol. I'm tea total from now on. But that's not going to stop me from eyeing up all those pretty WRAF's out there!" exclaimed Peter.

"You're mad! You can't keep your hands off those women, without some Dutch courage!" joked Gordon.

"That is true! But honestly, I'm not going to touch a drop of the hard stuff, I swear!" claimed Peter, with honesty.

"I'll believe that when I see it!" stated Alf, with tongue in cheek.

"Me too!" agreed Gordon facetiously.

"Come along with me then, and see for yourself!" replied Peter, calling their bluff.

"Nope, like I said earlier, I'm turning in early!" stated Alf categorically.

"And you're going to forfeit the chance, of pulling a lovely WRAF?" asked Peter.

"Yep! My health depends on it, mate! If I carry on like this, boozing my life away, I'll be dead in six months!" exclaimed Alf facetiously.

"You don't need to booze, to have fun!" stated Peter.

"That's all well and good saying that now. But when push comes to shove, inside the NAAFI bar, things are a lot different! The smell of the barmaid's apron, always leads me on to having a pint of lager, then another, and another, until bang! I've overdone it again. Nope, I'm staying well clear of alcohol, until at least I've got this course finished. It's far too dangerous to do anything otherwise," replied Alf.

"Okay, it's your loss, mate!" stated Peter.

"*It's my career, that's more important*!" replied Alf.

"Well, if you change your mind, let me know. As we are one short on the table football!" joked Clem.

"I'll play, but I'm not larking football all night!" stated Peter, in no uncertain terms.

"I'll lark too, mate, don't worry," enthused Gordon, warming to the idea of playing table football, and working it out in his head on how to take his revenge on Clem, after the last game.

"Great, so is that three playing?" asked Clem, in reply.

"Yep!" affirmed Peter.

"We need another to lark, to make it fair," said Clem.

"Just a minute, I'll ask Jack Pott, to see if he wants to play," piped up Gordon.

"Hang on! Hang on! Don't be too hasty! I'll lark," pleaded Alf.

"*I thought you said, you were having an early night,*" replied Clem.

"I've changed my mind," stated Alf.

"Okay, no worries," replied Clem. "But why the change of heart?"

"Cheers!" gasped Alf. "*It's because, I didn't fancy having toothpaste spread all over my nether regions!*"

"Eh? What do you mean, Alf?" asked Peter, butting in.

"Don't ask!" replied Alf.

"He's on about getting his balls smeared with Colgate, by us lot!" explained Gordon. "When he's fast asleep."

"Yes, that's correct! Because it bloody well stings!" admitted Alf.

"Have you experienced that before?" asked Clem.

"Not half I have, twice!" replied Alf, with a grimace. "At RAF Swinderby!" he revealed. "I was sleeping off another session of boozing, and dropped off to kip, at about nine o'clock in the evening, the following night, and in the morning, my balls seemed like they were on fire!" exclaimed Alf.

"What was it?" asked Clem.

"The buggers in my billet, had come in from the NAAFI, sloshed as hell, and they decided it would be fun to apply toothpaste, all over my bollocks, and man did it sting!" explained Alf.

"Ouch!" replied Clem.

"And if that wasn't enough, on the last night before my Passing Out parade, I decided on another early night, and damn, they did the same thing again, which was worse than the first one!" exclaimed Alf.

"Sorry, I shouldn't laugh, but it's blooming funny!" replied Clem, stifling a snigger.

"It's funny now, but it wasn't at the time," stated Alf.

"Okay, once bitten, but twice shy!" exclaimed Clem. "So then, to change the subject, I'll see you all later on lads, at say seven o'clock? Is that okay for the kick off time?" asked Clem, getting up from his chair.

"Yep, that's fine, I look forward to it, with relish!" replied Gordon.

"Is it the same teams as before?" asked Clem.

"*Oh yes, definitely*!" agreed Gordon, with a crafty glint in his eye.

"Sounds good to me! I'll see you all at seven o'clock!" exclaimed Clem leaving the other three airmen to finish off their meals.

Clem strolled back to the billet block, and was grateful that the rain had stopped. His mind was focused on getting across the road, without being knocked down, as the cars were moving in all different directions. After negotiating the busy road, that separated him from the billet block, Clem got back to his bed, in one piece.

He showered, changed clothes and laid back, to unwind. There was music playing in the billet room, which consisted of twelve airmen, all playing various tunes, and

Clem picked up numerous songs, from the different corners of the room, ranging from David Bowie, Abba and 10cc, to Stevie Wonder, Joan Armatrading and Steely Dan.

Clem enjoyed most music, and admired a lot of artists, such as Stevie Wonder, and he was seriously contemplating purchasing the double album, "Songs in the Key of Life," by Stevie Wonder, on cassette tape. In fact, it was on his shopping list, when he planned to visit the Hereford town centre, on Saturday. He had brought his cassette player with him, so it was just a matter of finding a music shop, so he could make that purchase.

Clem's music tastes varied greatly, from Status Quo, Bad Company and 10 cc, to Mud, Queen and Beatles, and from Thin Lizzy, Electric Light Orchestra and Bob Marley, to Chicago, Stevie Wonder and Four Tops. So it was very diverse. There wasn't any particular style of music that Clem could point to as his favourite, as he liked all sorts, including rock, pop, reggae, soul, country and western and disco. They were all as good as each other, in his estimation.

He listened contently to the various music tracks playing, and it made him very sleepy, in so much, that he could easily have dropped off to kip. But he knew that if he did that, he would nap for the rest of the evening, and miss the table football match. Clem held it together, fought the sleepiness and stayed awake. He was looking forward to visiting the NAAFI bar, and larking table football. But he was particularly enthusiastic about checking out the WRAF's, and especially the hot redhead, from the Airmen's Mess. He hoped she showed her face in the NAAFI bar, as he fancied getting to know her better, and that was without any alcohol, because Clem still wasn't old enough to drink, and after the mess the other airmen got themselves into last night, he was relieved he couldn't partake in the boozy sessions.

At five minutes to seven, Clem climbed off his bed, slipped on his shoes, put on his coat, and made tracks towards the NAAFI bar. He was in a rush, as he didn't want to turn up late, and be replaced by another trainee, as there would be plenty of other airmen that would jump at the chance to lark table football, and take his place, and that would have annoyed Clem immensely.

Clem arrived at the NAAFI bar at precisely 7pm, and the game was ready to start. He noticed that he had been replaced by Jack Pott, and before a ball was kicked, he rushed over to the table, to take his place in the two man team.

"Excuse me, Jack, *but that's my place you've taken*," stated Clem, catching his breath, after the short gallop he had just participated in, to reach the NAAFI bar on time.

"Eh, pardon? This is my place, mate!" replied Jack Pott, rather sharply.

"We didn't think you was turning up, Clem," piped up Alf, in a calming tone.

"Yeah, sorry. *But we did say seven o'clock, and it's exactly seven o'clock now*!" replied Clem.

"That's true, but we've invited Jack Pott to play, so it's a bit too late for you, mate," said Peter.

"I'm here on time. Not a ball has been kicked. It's seven o'clock. So, that's good enough for me to lark!" exclaimed Clem stubbornly.

"Yep, he's right! Let Clem play!" piped up Gordon, backing him fully, but having an ulterior motive for doing so, such as getting his revenge over Clem, after their last close-run game.

"Thank you, Gordon!" enthused Clem.

"Well, I suppose Clem did play the first game," stated Peter, in an amicable tone. "So it's only fair for him to continue playing! And it is seven o'clock, as we had stated, so he's not late. And we haven't kicked off yet," he added.

"Okay Clem, you can lark," stated Alf. "Welcome back into the team, pal!"

"Phew, cheers Alf, and sorry Jack," said Clem, trying to console a disappointed Jack Pott.

"No worries, I'll get over it, somehow, I suppose," replied Jack with tongue in cheek, playing down how gutted he really was.

"Better luck next time, Jack, but cheer up, you can be the referee!" joked Gordon.

"As if that's going to happen. The game runs itself. There are no fouls and no offsides, so I think I'll forget about being a ref, but I'll watch anyway," replied Jack, shrugging his shoulders.

"Good man!" enthused Clem, taking hold of the two control handles of the team in the blue kit, on the table football, that were operating the midfielders and strikers.

"Right, let play commence!" shouted Gordon keenly.

"May the best team win!" bellowed Alf.

"May that team be us!" yelled Peter.

Everyone had a little laugh to themselves at that last comment made by Peter, and then got down to some serious, highly concentrated table football play.

Clem notched the first goal after only five seconds, and followed it up two seconds later, with a carbon copy of the first goal, a thunderous shot from the centre forward. He was on top form, and whether it had anything to do with the elation he felt at being allowed to play, after the disappointment of being replaced by Jack Pott, he didn't know. But he clearly experienced a feeling of euphoria, when the other players decided it was only fair and proper that Clem should play, and it certainly had a telling effect on his morale. Clem played like a professional, with a cavalier attitude, and he had no restraints on the way he performed. He shot first time and on sight, and it was paying off, with dividends.

Clem claimed a quick-fire hat-trick after two minutes, to put him and Alf 3-0 up, and Gordon was fearing the worst, as he took full responsibility for all the three goals conceded, due to his inept play between the sticks. He had not got into the game yet, and his head was everywhere. Whether it was the thought of all those fit and hot WRAF's out there, in the RAF Hereford NAAFI world, or a reaction to the alcohol consumed last night, Gordon just could not put his finger on it. But he was determined to snap out of this daze, and try to make some stunning saves, to keep him and Peter Bird in the game. But the harder he tried, the worse it became, as Clem notched up another hat-trick in quick succession, to double the score, and make it 6-0, proving Clem's goal scoring prowess was second to none. Gordon's determination intensified, and he vowed to himself to make a success of this game, as he couldn't bear to lose again, and he made an instant impact by scoring a long range effort from defence, to bring the score to 6-1.

Clem was relaxed, cool, calm and collected and wasn't worried in the slightest. He merely controlled the ball in midfield and helped it on to his strikers, before unleashing another unstoppable shot into the back of the net, restoring their six goal cushion, and making the score 7-1. Alf was almost redundant in defence and in goal, as the ball did not get past the midfield, where Clem was so comfortably in control.

Gordon quickly had a thought about the way the match was going. He reckoned he was overworked in defence, and as the goalkeeper, and Peter had little or none of the ball, which wasn't what he had planned, or anticipated, so after a quickly taken decision, he opted on taking over the striker and midfield roles, and let Peter Bird have a go in goal, and with the very leaky defence, to see if that made any difference. Peter didn't like it, however.

"Huh? *What are you doing*?" questioned Peter, as Gordon commandeered the striker and midfield controls from Peter.

"I'm giving us a chance to win. I'm rubbish in defence! You're rubbish in attack! So let's swap and see what happens!" insisted Gordon, with a firm and serious tone.

The change of tactics was instantly successful. Gordon whipped the ball into the back of the net, to reduce the arrears, three seconds later, and he followed it up with another, eleven seconds after that. Peter was encouraged by this in goal, and made a string of successful saves to keep them in the game. The score stood at 7-3, and Gordon was a lot happier now than he had been a few minutes ago. He was even happier a minute later, when he claimed four goals in quick succession, and he was over the moon with the incredible transformation, seeing a six goal deficit reduced to nil. The score was now 7-7.

Peter continued with his great work in goal, and stopped a series of thunderous shots from Clem, which Gordon would probably have conceded, and it raised Gordon's morale tenfold. He shuffled the players from side to side in the forward line, feigned a shot, shuffled again, feigned another shot, and then blasted the ball hard into the corner of the goal, to put his side 8-7 up.

Clem was flabbergasted and didn't know what was going wrong. But he didn't panic. He merely played it cool, and continued to do what he had been doing, with verve, confidence and diligence, and his persistence paid off as he struck the goal of the game. He played the ball from his central midfielder to his striker in the middle, and without hesitation, and in a split second, he drove a magnificent shot home, to restore parity, with an equaliser. 8-8.

The game ebbed and flowed, from one side of the pitch to the other. Clem had chances, but was off target. Gordon also could have scored on two or three occasions, but he spurned his chances too, and the match was locked, at eight all.

Clem tried all he knew, but was unsuccessful. Gordon tried varied stuff, but still couldn't break the deadlock. Peter was organised in defence, and thorough with his reading of the game. It was going to take something extraordinary, to separate these two teams.

Chance after chance came and went, but neither Clem nor Gordon could take advantage. It was tense, nerve-wracking and too close for comfort. Clem wanted to win to continue his unbroken winning streak, Alf wasn't too bothered, but Peter and Gordon were desperate to grab hold of a victory, to experience the sweet taste of success, for the very first time. And when Peter slammed in a long range shot from defence, putting them 9-8 ahead, it looked like their wishes were going to come true. But Clem had other ideas on the agenda, and before Gordon and Alf could blink, Clem slotted home another goal to equalise, and make the score 9-9.

"Next goal wins, eh?" suggested Clem.

"Yep, as the beer's getting warm!" exclaimed Peter, in reply.

"Excuse me, you said you weren't drinking!" exclaimed Clem.

"I'm not, I was just saying the beer's getting warm!" replied Peter, with tongue in cheek.

"You're itching for a pint, aren't you?" piped up Alf.

"Aren't we all?" replied Peter.

"Nope, I'm not. I'm finished with booze, for now!" bellowed Gordon.

"Me too!" agreed Alf.

"Come on then, let's play this match!" exclaimed Clem impatiently.

The table football game resumed, and Peter seemed in a rush to finish it, as he slammed a stunning shot from the left full back towards the goal, and Alf just managed to block it at the last second. He cleared the ball out of the danger zone, and Clem controlled with a touch of finesse, hesitated a short while to bamboozle his opponents, before striking a sweet shot towards the target. It zoomed past Gordon in midfield, and was too quick for Peter's defensive players, but he just managed to save with his goalkeeper, for a stunning block.

Alf and Clem covered their faces in agony, as they were certain that was going in, but alas, it was not to be, and they had to continue playing.

The save by Peter in goal spurred on Gordon upfront, and when he received the ball from the goalkeeper's clearance, he had the goal at his mercy, as Alf had momentarily lost concentration, after that last gasp save by Peter, and he was not ready. But Gordon hadn't noticed, and he was too slow to take advantage, and he fluffed his chance to score the winner. Clem gasped a sigh of relief at that lost opportunity by Gordon, and he reckoned that if it had been Peter, then it would be all over now, because he knew Peter wouldn't have squandered a chance like that.

Clem had a chance to win the game, a couple of seconds later, but he too fluffed his opportunity to score, when he slammed the ball against the post. The ball rebounded out, and landed at one of Gordon's central midfield players, and he poked a seemingly tame effort towards Alf in goal, and it trickled in, to give Gordon and Peter an amazing win, by 10 goals to 9.

"Well played you two," stated Clem, in a tone of calm composure, hiding the fact that he was bitterly disappointed to lose the match. He was a sore loser and didn't deny it, but he gave praise when it was due.

"Yes I reiterate that! Congrats on a fine win!" exclaimed Alf, in a couldn't care less sort of attitude, as he wasn't really bothered if he won or lost.

"Cheers guys!" replied Gordon.

"Yes thanks. It was nip and tuck all the way, to the last goal!" piped up Peter.

Both Gordon and Peter were beaming inside, and were ecstatic as can be, but they saw how much Clem was hurting, so they didn't rub it in too much. They knew the boot could have been on the other foot, and they would have been just as gutted to have lost out, especially after their great comeback, but that was football.

"Are we larking again?" asked Gordon hopefully.

"Maybe," replied Clem, through gritted teeth.

"Yes, I'm sure we will," stated Alf, shrugging his shoulders, with indifference. He wasn't bothered if they did or they didn't.

"Great!" enthused Gordon.

"It'll give you a chance of revenge, eh?" stated Peter.

"I'm not bothered about any revenge. It's just a game to me, a fun game at that!" replied Alf, with honesty.

"We'll see," stated Clem with a downcast attitude, still trying to come to terms with the defeat.

"Okay, let's go and sniff out all those WRAF's then. I'm sure they'll be plenty to keep us occupied," said Peter.

"What about a pint?" asked Alf.

"Nope!" exclaimed Gordon.

"Are you kidding?" said Peter.

"I'm deadly serious! I need one to drown my sorrows!" joked Alf, with tongue in cheek. "What about you Clem, are you interested in a pint or two?" asked Alf.

"No, I wouldn't if I could mate, I hate the stuff! It's nothing but poison, in my estimation!" exclaimed Clem.

"*So, that's a no, then*?" replied Alf facetiously.

When Clem looked up, he spotted the hot red-headed female from the Airmen's Mess. She was dancing to the track, "The Soul City Walk" sung by Archie Bell and the Drells, and she was enjoying every second of it. Clem watched her moving to the music, and was impressed. She could certainly throw some shapes, in a funky sort of way. When the music stopped playing, she went back to her chair with a group of other WRAF's, and helped herself to a drink, from a half pint glass, that was sitting on the table. Clem was tempted to stroll coolly over to her, to say hello. But she suddenly burst into floods of tears, and sobbed her heart out uncontrollably.

"Hey, is that your girlfriend over there, weeping?" asked Alf.

"Yes, it looks like it, but how did you know I liked her?" replied Clem.

"Because your tongue is hanging out, everytime you look at her!" said Alf.

"Oh, am I that obvious? Crikey, I'd be a rubbish spy!" replied Clem.

"Go over there and console her!" exclaimed Alf.

"Nah, now's not the right time, if she's upset. As I haven't even introduced myself yet," replied Clem.

"Oh, okay then. Please yourself," stated Alf.

Clem looked across at the hot, red-headed WRAF, and hoped she was okay. But he didn't bother to enquire on her welfare. He let her half a dozen new friends, the other WRAF's, take care of her, but he continued to monitor the situation.

"She's lost her grandmother!" yelped one of the hot redhead's friends.

"Awww!" came the reply from the other WRAF's around her, and Clem stayed silent, although he was deeply concerned, and felt sorry for the red-headed WRAF.

"Bless you!" shouted one of the other WRAF's nearby.

The hot red-headed female was consoled by the other WRAF's, before slowly walking out of the NAAFI bar and away to her billet block, for some privacy. Clem didn't even acknowledge her, as she shuffled past, as he was unsure what to do. But she hadn't seen Clem anyway, as her head was down, and her eyes were full of the tears of sorrow.

Clem shrugged his shoulders. He had been ready to chat her up. But after the sombre scenes, with the sadness of losing her grandmother, Clem's gut feeling told him to hang fire on chatting her up, and that it would be better to wait, until she had come to terms with the shocking news.

"What are you going to do next Clem, now that your girlfriend's disappeared?" asked Alf.

"I'll look around, and see what else there is," replied Clem.

"You cruel so and so! If I was you, I'd go and follow her, to see if she's okay," suggested Alf.

"Nah. The vibe's not right. The chemistry's not there. She isn't going to be wanting to chat and smooch, after losing her grandma," replied Clem.

"I'd have at least asked her, if she was okay," suggested Alf.

"*She didn't even see me*!" replied Clem.

"That's no excuse! Wish her well, console her. That's what women like," said Alf.

"Maybe I've got a lot to learn, about what makes a woman tick!" replied Clem.

"And I thought you were the expert and all that, with your Sociology O Level, grade A!" quipped Alf.

"I thought I was too. So it just goes to show, we are forever learning," replied Clem.

"Yep, we live and learn!" agreed Alf.

Clem continued watching the dancing females shaking their thing, and they were getting down to some serious grooving, when "Play That Funky Music," starting playing loudly, and it filled the dance floor with the bodies of the hot, energetic WRAFs, of all shapes and sizes. They continued to move to the beat, with incredible finesse, and it didn't alter when "You Should Be Dancing," by the Bee Gees, began to play. This was followed by "You To Me Are Everything," by the Real Thing, and the WRAFs gyrated, twisted and grinded to the disco music.

Clem was fascinated, with the way in which the women seemed to love to flirt, with their curvy bodies on show, and their figures were well worth an eyeful, as their tight tee shirts, short skirts and shapely legs, were well in abundance, and Clem was spoilt for choice, on where to feast his eyes.

His attention was caught by a curvaceous and busty WRAF, dressed in a tight, black, knee length pencil skirt, and tapered white blouse, with frills and tassels, and it was Clem that was getting all the thrills, by eyeing her up. He made eye contact with the female, which was steamy, passionate and rivetting. He couldn't take his eyes off her breasts, that were bulging inside her blouse, and her shapely arse, that was round and large. It looked as juicy as a peach.

Clem watched her boogie to the tracks being played, including "Blinded By The Light," by Manfred Mann, "The Best Disco In Town," by the Ritchie Family, "Heaven Must Be Missing An Angel," by Tavares and "Disco Duck," by Rick Dees And His Cast Of Idiots.

Clem liked all those songs, and the ones before them, that had been played, and he was tempted to go and ask the lady for a dance. But something stopped him. A gut feeling, and he didn't know why. But he obeyed his instincts, and stayed put. He turned round to look for his three friends, but they were not there. He noticed that they had all gone to the bar, to order a pint.

"*So much then, for them not drinking alcohol*," thought Clem. But the lure of the Dutch Courage, proved too hard to ignore.

Clem tutted to himself, at their change of heart. He couldn't understand why they were risking their RAF careers. But something had made them do it, and the smell of the barmaid's apron had a great deal to do with it, or was that the smell of the WRAF's perfume? Either way, the three airmen, Alf King, Gordon Bottle and Peter Bird were thirstily sinking lagers, in a pint sized glass, with a fervent appetite.

"You'll be sorry in the morning!" exclaimed Clem, as the three trainees approached him on the edge of the dance floor, and they shrugged their shoulders, with a couldn't care less sort of attitude.

"Tomorrow never comes!" replied Alf, with tongue in cheek.

"True, but the training course does," answered Clem facetiously.

"Ah, I'll be okay, as I'm only having the one," piped up Gordon.

"You said you weren't having any!" stated Clem.

"I'm feeling like I deserve one, after today. As it's been very fraught!" said Peter.

"Yes, that's because you were drunk last night, and are hung over today! The cause of that fraughtness is in the palm of your hand!" stated Clem, pointing at the lager in his glass.

"The hair of the dog!" replied Alf.

"Yeah, yeah, yeah! I get it! *But make sure it isn't the hair of a dozen dogs, like last night!"* joked Clem, shaking his head.

"Maybe it will, maybe it won't. Who knows? It's all about today. I'm enjoying myself, and that's all that counts. Tomorrow can take care of itself!" replied Gordon.

"Here here! I agree!" seconded Alf.

"Me too!" agreed Peter. "We are a long time dead!" he added, then taking a long gulp of the lager from his glass, he finished his pint.

"I think you should join in Clem, and have a pint, and stop acting like my grandmother!" joked Gordon.

"Maybe I should. But not until I'm eighteen, which isn't too far away now, only two months, and then I shall see what all this fuss is about!" exclaimed Clem.

"Good man! You won't be disappointed, and it might even help you talk to the opposite sex!" joked Alf facetiously.

Clem stood on the peripheral of the dance floor, and looked for the hot, busty WRAF, with the tight, black pencil skirt and large arse, but she was nowhere to be seen. He wondered where she had disappeared to. "As she was tasty," thought Clem, and as he fancied the pants off her, he reckoned a smooch wouldn't go amiss. A slow song was playing and many of the WRAF's had paired themselves up with an horny airman, and some shenanigans were taking place, with the majority of the dancing couples.
Clem still hadn't found the nerve to approach a WRAF, never mind dancing with one. He was in need of some Dutch courage, but resisted all temptation to drink alcohol, in case he ended up paralytic, and was kicked off the training course. He watched his three airmen colleagues, Alf, Peter and Gordon sinking pint after pint after pint, and not relenting, before they ventured out on to the heaving, sweaty dance floor, to grab a WRAF, and join in with the high-spirited behaviour. They all managed to find a willing female, that was ready to have some fun.
Clem continued to observe the dancing couples, that were swaying from side to side, but he still hadn't spotted the busty WRAF, with the lovely large arse. He kept his eyes

peeled for her, as he still fancied a smooch, even though he had a strange gut feeling about her.

He decided he couldn't hang around waiting all night, so he decided to take the plunge and try his hand at a smooch with another WRAF. He took a long, deep breath and tested the water, and struck lucky first time, with a diminutive blonde woman, displaying a sensual smile and a cracking pair of tits. Clem piled in and grabbed the female by her hips and held her tightly, as the music was playing slowly and sexily. The track in question was "If You Leave Me Now," by Chicago. The blonde WRAF clutched Clem tightly and pushed her heaving breasts into him, and Clem felt them rubbing against his chest. It was a very scintillating moment, as Clem had never had that experience before in all his seventeen years, and he liked it. He placed his hands on her waist, and wanted to feel her arse, but he decided not to push his luck too far.

He played it cool, and had no idea if that was the right thing to do, or not. But he didn't care. He went with the flow. He did whatever came into his head, and he enjoyed every second of it. Having a female in his arms, that looked good, smelled good and when his mouth met hers, tasted good too, it was the stuff of dreams. Her lipstick was strawberry flavoured, and it drove Clem wild with passion. Who needed alcohol to produce Dutch courage? The taste of the blonde WRAF's mouth and the smell of her perfume, mixed with the aroma of her perspiring body, was ten times more intoxicating than alcohol, reckoned Clem, and it had him floating on cloud nine. He felt great.

The next track began to play, and fortunately for Clem it was another slow one, for an extended smooch. The blonde female liked it too and pulled Clem even closer to her. The magical track in question was "Love And Affection," by

Joan Armatrading. It got Clem further into the romantic groove, and it turned on the blonde WRAF, who grinded and rubbed her crotch against Clem's genitals.

Clem and the blonde WRAF, with the sensual smile and captivating perfume, were at it like randy rabbits, in the centre of the lust filled dance floor, kissing, fondling, groping and having the very amorous time of their lives.

Another slow track began to play, to keep the snogathon couple busy, and it was "I'm Not In Love," by 10cc. A very passionate, carnal and arousing track, even if the title of the song was somewhat contradictory of itself, as both Clem and the blonde WRAF were most definitely showing some kind of love to one another, in a crude sort of manner. They were oblivious to what was happening around them, as their lips locked together, like super glue. It must have been their lucky day, because another slow track began to play, to encourage the loving couple to remain on the dance floor, and Clem and the blonde WRAF, along with a dozen other lustful couples, smooched to the sound of "Misty Blue," by Dorothy Moore, followed by "Kiss And Say Goodbye," by The Manhattans. The couple were in Seventh Heaven, and continued to be oblivious to everything around them, and Clem was thoroughly enjoying this close contact smooching, and wanted it to go on forever. Then the lights went on, and the music stopped. It was closing time.

Clem was startled and appeared dumbstruck, like he had just woken up from a deep sleep, and he wondered where he was. It was as if he had been dreaming all of this. He looked around the place, and for a moment or two, he forgot where he was, *and he hadn't touched a drop of alcohol*. He looked at the blonde WRAF, and he suddenly realised where he was, and he was impressed by the look of her, as she was a very attractive young lady. But before he could introduce himself in a polite manner, she rushed off into the throng of the crowd, and disappeared into thin air. Clem sighed with disappointment, but wouldn't forget the thrill of his very first smooch, with an amorous and desirable WRAF. He was still daydreaming about her, when he was greeted by his three friends, on the edge of the dance floor.

"Saw you! Saw you! You dirty stop out!" exclaimed Alf.
"What?" asked Clem.
"Copping off with that WRAF!" replied Alf.
"Yep, who needs alcohol to make out with a sexy young lady?" quipped Clem.
"Eh, you mean to say, you never had a pint or two, for some Dutch courage?" asked Gordon.
"Yep, I haven't touched a drop of the hard stuff!" exclaimed Clem proudly.
"Wow, you've done well! She was a bit of alright, too," replied Peter.
"Thanks! But it was only a random choice. I took the plunge and struck lucky!" enthused Clem.
"Yep, it's a lot like a lucky bag. You're not sure what you're going to get, when you enter the dance floor, with the lights down, until it's too late!" stated Alf.
"That's true! But with her sensual smile, eager hands, provocative perspiring aroma, mixed with Chanel Number Five perfume, and the slow swaying, sultry movements of a smooching lady in my arms, it's a lot like paradise!" exclaimed Clem.
"Yep, and I take it you're smitten with her?" replied Alf.
"I'm smitten with her smell, she smelled gorgeous!" exclaimed Clem.
"*Yep, it's love!*" stated Gordon, with tongue in cheek.

"Give over, I've only just met her!" replied Clem, blushing profusely.

"And now she's disappeared into the night!" exclaimed Alf.

"Yep!" agreed Clem. "You've got it spot on!"

"Never mind, mate. There's plenty of fish in the sea!" piped up Peter enthusiastically, hoping to ease Clem's disappointment.

"Give over pal. He's got another WRAF on the back-burner!" revealed Alf.

"Have you really, Clem? Well, you're a dark horse, aren't you?" joked Peter.

"It's nothing really. I'm just doing what comes naturally, and all without the dependence of alcohol," stated Clem.

"I'll have to try that!" slurred Alf drunkenly.

"Yep, me too. It'll save on the beer money!" exclaimed Gordon greedily.

"I agree, and it will be easier on my head, in the morning," piped up Peter, looking for sympathy.

"And more importantly, *you'll remember what happened*!" joked Clem, with tongue in cheek.

"Hey, you might be on to something there, Clem," admitted Alf.

"I've got to try it," stated Gordon.

"Me too. It's worth a shot," agreed Peter.

Clem strode proudly away with his three friends, towards the airmen's billet block, with the comfort of knowing that his pure bravery was ten times stronger than alcohol, when it came to finding Dutch courage, and he would choose those tactics again. He had been well and truly initiated into the "Smooch with a WRAF Club," and was as pleased as punch. He was particularly impressed with himself, in regard to proving himself with a WRAF, after all the

Mickey taking about him being too scared to chat to the women. It had shut his three colleagues up, once and for all.

When Clem got back to the billet block, he fell asleep as soon as his head hit the pillow. He was shattered and slept like a top. When he awoke in the morning, he was full of the joys of Spring. His head didn't ache. He had no hangover. But his stomach was rumbling, and his chin was in need of a good shave, as the stubble was growing through thickly like on a tramp's face, and he didn't want kicking off the course, for being unkempt and scruffy. So, the first task of the day was to have a shave. He showered too. His mind was filled between three WRAFs. The red head, the blonde and the one he had a weird gut feeling about. He was spoilt for choice. He decided to forget about them now, and think about having something to eat.

Breakfast for Clem was as good as it always had been. He wasn't disappointed. He spotted Alf, Gordon and Peter on the next table and they were tucking in to their food, like it was going out of fashion.

"You're *scoffing* loads!" yelled Clem, in the direction of the three airmen.

"Yep, it's a tip I got from my grandmother years ago.....She told me, anytime I happen to get drunk, the best remedy for an hangover, is plenty of greasy food, such as the Great British fry up, with all the trimmings, including as many slices of bacon, sausages, eggs, tomatoes and fried bread as possible, to soak up the beer!" exclaimed Alf, with a shrug of his shoulders in uncertainty. He wasn't sure if it would work or not, but he was giving it a go.

Gordon Bottle and Peter Bird believed in Alf's grandmother's tip, and they both gobbled up a massive cooked breakfast, to help them in their quest to be fit and ready for a tough day in the Training Centre. They had pinned all their hopes on Alf's gran's, handy, hangover, remedy.

Half an hour later, the four airmen trooped into the classroom with the other ten trainees, to face another day in the stifling conditions of the RAF Hereford Supply Trade Training Centre. Alf soon felt the benefit of the greasy cooked breakfast, as did Gordon. But Peter still hadn't fully recovered from last night, and was feeling a little queasy, under the weather and his eyes were sensitive to the light. He reckoned it would wear off in the course of the day, but his headache was getting worse, as the minutes ticked by.

"Good morning trainees!" bellowed Corporal McCauley brightly. "How is everyone?"

"Very good, corporal!" replied the fourteen airmen, including Peter, who was lying through his back teeth. He wasn't feeling well at all. In fact he was feeling worse than yesterday, but he didn't say anything to anyone. He was counting on the food he had consumed to begin soaking up the excess alcohol, and there had been plenty of it, to assist him in clearing his sore head. He knew if Corporal McCauley twigged onto his condition, he would be out on his ear, in disgrace.

Although the day at RAF Hereford Supply Trade Training Centre went well for Clem. The same couldn't be said for Peter "Squeaky" Bird. He was struggling all day, but somehow kept his hangover a secret. He didn't let on to anybody about his ailment with the ale, and soldiered on, with the mother of all hangovers, although he wasn't sure if Corporal McCauley had worked it out. He didn't say anything to Peter, and probably gave him the benefit of the doubt, so it was a welcome relief to him, but he vowed never to touch another drop of alcohol, for the rest of the training course, *again*. He was adamant he'd stick by his word. He liked the idea of pulling a WRAF with pure bravery, which Clem had demonstrated, with his success on the dance floor, with the bird with the blonde hair, so Peter decided to follow suit and much preferred to be safe than sorry. He didn't fancy being sent home early either, and having to explain to his parents that it was all down to alcohol. But if he had carried on with the drunken evenings in the NAAFI bar, that's exactly what would have happened, and he would have found it difficult to live it down.

It was Friday night. The RAF station was preparing for the weekend. Not many trainees had hung around, except for Clem, Alf and Peter. The other eleven airmen on the supply trade training course went home for the weekend.

"So, it looks like it's just the three of us, then," stated Clem, settling down to tuck into his tea in the Airman's Mess, half an hour later.

"Yep, we can't even play table football, as we are one short," replied Alf, chewing on a tasty rump steak.

"Never mind, I prefer a break from that anyway. It can become monotonous, if played too much," piped up Peter, sipping at his lukewarm cup of tea.

"Yep, you're right," agreed Clem.

"So, what's it going to be?" asked Alf.

"I don't know. Most of the WRAFs have cleared off, so there'll be no smooching!" moaned Peter.

"No they haven't! There's a few over there, in the corner!" exclaimed Clem, noticing the redhead was still around, along with the WRAF that he had a gut feeling about. But there was no sign of the blonde WRAF, with the sensual smile.

"*So, what is it tonight?*" asked Alf impatiently.

"Television, I reckon! Let's see what's on the box!" suggested Clem.

"Okay, that sounds good! I haven't watched television for ages. It'll make a fine change," agreed Peter.

"*Yes, and you might even stay sober*!" exclaimed Clem, with tongue in cheek.

"True! So, let's meet back at the NAAFI bar at around seven, and then head over to the Television Room. There should be something decent to watch on around that time," stated Alf.

"Alright, seven o'clock it is!" replied Clem.

The three airmen finished their meal and headed back to the billet block, to shower and change, then unwind for a short while. Clem bought a newspaper on his way out of the Airmen's Mess, to be able to check on the sports pages later on, but when he got back to his bed and flicked through the paper, there wasn't much news to get excited about. He put the newspaper down on his bedside cabinet and waited patiently for seven o'clock.

The billet block was so quiet, with most of the airmen away on weekend leave. It was nice and peaceful. There was no music playing. It was just silent and it made a great change. At seven o'clock, Clem got up to meet his two friends at the NAAFI bar, and when they all grouped together, they headed to the Television Room.

"Great stuff, the Muppets are on!" enthused Alf, as he switched on the television set.

There was nobody else present in the Television Room at that time, but as the three airmen began to settle down, the room slowly began to fill up, and there were more trainees on the RAF station grounds than Clem, Alf and Peter had bargained for. The room became quite full. Clem even noticed that the redhead who had caught his eye a couple of days ago was present, and she had in tow with her, a clinging, randy airman, with hands like an octopus. They were necking and cavorting on the front row of the Television Room, in full view of the rest of the trainees, with no shame.

"Hey look Clem, there's that red headed bird of yours, with another fella!" stated Alf.

"Yep, I've seen her. So much for her, *being my girlfriend*!" replied Clem.

"Never mind mate! At least you've got another one on the back burner!" chirped Alf in support.

"Yes, that's true. There's always plenty of fish in the sea!" exclaimed Clem.

"There sure is, *as you can testify*!" piped up Peter.

"Yes, and I wonder what she's up to this weekend?" asked Clem in a dreamy tone, with dreamy eyes, daydreaming about the sensual blonde.

"Who knows?" asked Peter.

"*Who cares*?" joked Alf facetiously.

"You're right, who cares? Live for the moment is my motto, and that's exactly what I'm going to do!" bellowed Clem, with a tone of determination.

"Sure, that's the way Clem! If you can smooch with a WRAF, without the support of alcohol, you can do anything mate!" stated Alf.

"Anyway, shush now! As I can't hear anything!" ordered Peter, pointing to the Muppets television programme, on the TV set.

"Alright, alright! It's only the flipping Muppets!" snapped Alf.

"Yes, well, I'm enjoying it!" replied Peter, shuffling excitedly in his seat.

"Leave him Alf. He's *living for the moment*!" joked Clem.

"Yeah Clem, that's right!" agreed Peter. "You've got it spot on!"

Clem and Alf laughed, along with Peter, at that funny quip, and they all turned to face the television screen to enjoy the Muppet Show, and whatever capers they were likely to get up to. Clem put the thought of the sexy redhead out of his mind and focused on the television screen. He even dismissed the blonde WRAF from all his thoughts, but he still had the WRAF that gave him a weird gut feeling, nestling inside his head. And he didn't know why.

The airmen and airwomen guffawed and screamed with laughter, at the comedy presented to them, on the Muppet Show. It was hilarious. Clem had never watched this show before and was surprised that he got so enthralled in it. It was very cleverly scripted, he thought, and had some great comical moments. It cheered him up no end, after the devastating sight of seeing what he thought was his girlfriend having her face snogged off by another airman. But that was the cruelty of life. It had happened to him before, in 1974, when his then girlfriend, Janet, two timed him, so this was no real surprise. It was just the way the cookie crumbled, and was part of the fabric of life.

After the Muppet Show had ended, Clem was wondering what was going to be shown next. The room had filled up to capacity and there was a lot of noise, as everyone aired their views on the previous programme, and most of the opinions were a positive one. The reaction had been welcoming.

After a commercial break for a couple of minutes, as the channel was tuned into ITV, the next programme began and it was the Benny Hill Show, with lots of innuendo, saucy antics, scantily clad dancing women and double-entendre. It was funny, but cringeworthy funny, and it had always been a favourite of Clem's, since he was 14 years of age. It was titillating and eye opening, and a few of the viewing trainees were squirming in their seats, with embarrassment. But it was good, clean fun, thought Clem, and he laughed heartily at the sketches performed admirably by Benny Hill and his associates, who were experts in slapstick, visual comedy and farce.

When the Benny Hill Show finished, Clem didn't think anything could top it. But he was wrong, because the next programme being shown was Starsky and Hutch, an American cop drama, with intrigue, twists, a good plot and some intricate comedy action. It was an entertaining watch and one that Clem thoroughly enjoyed. He was thankful someone had switched it over, as it was aired on the BBC, and when Clem glanced across at his two friends, to give the thumbs up sign, he realised that it was Alf that had commandeered the remote control, and was dictating what was being watched, as he fiddled with the digital technology.

"Hey, it's you that's got the controls!" exclaimed Clem.

"Yep!" replied Alf.

"How did you manage that?" asked Clem.

"Well, we were the first in here, so I just grabbed the box and carried on picking my favourite programmes," explained Alf.

"Good thinking!" stated Clem.

"Yep, it's our prerogative, first in, first served, with the television programmes," quipped Alf.

"That's only right, I'd say, mate," agreed Clem.

"Yes, somebody has to decide on what we watch, and make sure we have quality, so I thought I'd do the job," stated Alf, with a crafty smile.

"Nice one," piped up Peter.

"I'll remember that, the next time I'm in here!" exclaimed Clem.

"You've got to make sure *you're here first,* though," replied Alf.

"Yep, of course. That stands to reason," agreed Clem.

News at Ten followed Starsky and Hutch, and the chatting in the Television Room began again, in earnest. There wasn't much interest in the news, and as Clem had already found out by flicking through the morning paper, he could see why, because there wasn't much news to be offered.

At half past ten, Alf flicked the channel over from BBC to ITV again, and was just in time to catch the start of the Friday night feature, "Appointment With Fear," a regular weekly offering for horror fans, and tonight's picture was "The Bride of Frankenstein." Clem wasn't too fussed with horror films, but stayed and watched, and treated it like a comedy, in the Benny Hill mould, with chills.

The room was filled with gasps, shrieks and screams, and that was just from the airmen in the audience. The WRAFs put on a braver face and hid their fear under their hands, as they covered their faces. Clem remembered when he was little, and how scared he was when he watched Dr Who. He normally hid behind the settee when the Daleks came on. It was their voices that frightened him the most, and it sent shivers of fear down his spine. He didn't have nightmares. He was just scared during the show, but he still watched the programme every week, and reckoned he liked being frightened. Even the theme tune at the beginning of the show was scary, thought Clem, although he was only around five years old at the time. This movie tonight, "The Bride of Frankenstein," wasn't as scary as Dr Who, thought Clem. Nothing could beat the Daleks for "scare-ability." They were the best at putting the frighteners on, bar none, and Clem reckoned he would be supported by millions of people who would agree with him.

When the film finished at half past twelve in the morning, the National Anthem played and everyone stood to attention, before making tracks back to their respective billets.

Clem slept well and didn't stir whatsoever during the night, and he wasn't sure why that was. Maybe it was because there was nobody in his billet room, and it provided him with a "snoring free" environment. But whatever the reason, it offered him a fantastic night's rest and he kipped until 9 am, which was a good two or three hours more than his usual sleeping pattern provided, during the last five days. But he knew how much he needed it, as his brain was frazzled, with the daily intake of new information, from the supply trade training course.

It was Saturday morning, and Clem wasn't sure what time breakfast started or finished. Nobody had informed him. Corporal McCauley hadn't mentioned it, nor had his two colleagues, Alf or Peter, so Clem was none the wiser. But he didn't care. "This wasn't a hotel," thought Clem. "It was an RAF training base, and meals would be served as and when the times were stipulated," although those times hadn't yet been identified by Clem.

Clem showered and dressed in civvy clothes of black jeans, blue checked Ben Sherman shirt, blue woolly jumper, black brogues and a black Harrington waist length jacket. He headed out of the billet, and was confronted by rain and sleet on his arrival outside. It wasn't the ideal weather for a walk, but Clem knew that it had to be done, as RAF Hereford didn't operate Room Service. With the rain quite persistent, and falling very quickly, Clem decided a sprint was the best thing to do, to avoid catching pneumonia. He reached the Airmen's Mess in a time of three minutes and two seconds, which was a new world record for Clem, in all the trips he had made there. He was still soaked to the skin though, as it was the sort of rain that just hung in the air and was like a wall of water, which just drenched everything, whether you were in it for long, or not. But it didn't bother Clem. At least the Airmen's Mess was open. He checked on the information board that had pinned to it the opening times, and he read it with interest.

"Ah," sighed Clem. "Open from seven in the morning, until seven in the evening, all day long. Cool!"

He tucked in to his breakfast, that consisted of four sausages, two slices of bacon, a scoop of beans, two stewed tomatoes and two fried eggs. He was famished, and as he had planned to visit Hereford town centre later, he was making sure he ate well now, just in case the food in the town was expensive. It was what his dad would have called, "forward planning."

There was no sign of either Alf or Peter, and Clem was wondering where they had got to. He hadn't arranged anything with them in regard to a shopping trip, but he was prepared to invite both of them along, to see if they fancied a jaunt into town.

He continued tucking in to his delicious fried breakfast, and chased it down with a warm, milky cup of tea. By the time he had finished, there was still no sign of the guys, so he reckoned he would be venturing into town on his own, then as he got up to take his pots away to the counter for washing, he was confronted with Alf and Peter, in a somewhat dishevelled state.

Clem looked at them, and almost fell about the place in hysterics. He had to hold his mouth tightly, to stop himself from laughing his head off.

"*Where are you two going?*" Clem asked.

"Work, training, or whatever it's called," replied Alf nonchalantly.

"*Work, training or whatever it's called?*" asked Clem, with tongue in cheek.

"Yep, but why is the Airmen's Mess so empty?" asked Alf, rubbing the sleep out of his eyes, and yawning.

"*Because it's Saturday!*" exclaimed Clem, in reply.

"You're kidding me!" shrieked Alf, turning red with embarrassment.

"Nope, it's true," stated Clem, trying to control his laughter.

Alf looked at Peter and Peter looked at Alf, and they didn't know whether to laugh or cry.

"Why didn't you tell me it was Saturday?" bellowed Alf, in the direction of Peter.

"I didn't know what day it was, to be honest. I just got up like normal, put on my uniform and headed to your room," replied Peter.

"Well dumbo, it's gash information, isn't it, you idiot!" screamed Alf.

"To be honest, it's a good job that it is Saturday, as it's saved your bacon! Because if you had turned up for the training course now, you would have been kicked off it for being late, as it's nearly ten o'clock," stated Clem, coolly, calmly and collectedly.

"Really?" asked Alf, staring daggers at Peter with fury.

"Don't blame me, because your watch has stopped! Just because I don't bother with one!" exclaimed Peter in his defence.

"Eh, you don't wear a watch?" asked Clem, looking at Peter with a puzzled expression.

"Yep, I can't wear one, as it brings me out in a terrible rash," explained Peter.

"Does it really? So how do you tell the time then?" asked Clem.

"At home, by the use of the radio. But here I've got an alarm clock, and use that, and then when I'm out, it's the clocks on the walls," explained Peter further.

"*When your alarm clock decides to work!*" exclaimed Alf sarcastically.

"Oh yes, I forgot to wind it up last night, as I was that knackered, and it failed to go off!" stated Peter, with tongue in cheek.

"Well, no harm done, eh. All's well that ends well," replied Clem jovially.

The two airmen nodded, and went to the serving hatch to pick up their breakfasts. Clem waited for them and strolled back to his table. He had nothing else to do. The two trainees returned five minutes later, with ample food on their plates, which was enough to feed the five thousand.

"Are you sure you've sufficient there lads?" joked Clem.

"*What do you mean? Don't you think there's enough here?*" replied Alf, rising from his seat, in preparation to return to the serving hatch for more.

"Hang on a minute mate! I was only joking!" exclaimed Clem. "Come back!"

"So was I!" replied Alf with tongue in cheek, and sitting back down again.

"I was going to say! I thought I had a lot piled on my plate, but you've doubled my serving!" joked Clem again, facetiously.

"Well, you never know when you're going to eat again, and besides that, the prices in town might be phenomenal," stated Alf.

"That was my exact reasoning too," replied Clem, nodding his head in agreement.

"Too right, as well," stated Alf, in no uncertain terms.

"So, what's your plans for afterwards?" asked Clem.

"Me? I'm off out into town!" exclaimed Alf. "What about you?"

"Me too. I was just about to ask you, if you wanted to join me for a jaunt around the shops," replied Clem.

"Yes, absolutely! I need some fresh air and a chance to stretch my legs, after being cooped up inside a classroom all week!" stated Alf.

"Good, good. What about you Peter?" asked Clem.

"What about me?" replied Peter.

"Regarding your plans for later. What are you up to?" asked Clem.

"Dunno, anything will do, as long as it doesn't involve consuming alcohol!" replied Peter.

"Okay, you can rest assured, I won't be indulging in beer drinking. But I can't speak for Alf," stated Clem.

"Nope, I'm on the wagon. No beer for me either!" exclaimed Alf, with a cheesy grin.

"So, are you joining us then, Peter?" asked Clem.

"Yep, I'll partake in whatever you're getting up to," agreed Peter.

"Good, we are off into town for a look around," stated Alf.

"Nice one, I'm sure I need a few things. So it'll give me an opportunity to buy them," replied Peter.

"Including a new alarm clock, eh, Peter?" joked Clem.

"Erm, no, not really. As that was entirely my fault, not the alarm clock's," replied Peter.

"And, you'll be buying a new watch, Alf?" asked Clem.

"Nope, that was my fault too, not the watch's, as I forgot to wind it up," replied Alf.

"So, that's two new brains and two memories, to put down on your shopping lists instead!" exclaimed Clem, with tongue in cheek.

"Nah, not a brain or a memory for me, thanks. Just time off needed to re-charge my batteries, as all this stress of learning is wearing me out!" replied Alf.

"And time off to help me recover, from my hangover," piped up Peter.

"That's it in a nutshell, your boozing!" stated Clem.

"Yeah well, I've given up on that," insisted Alf.

"And me too," agreed Peter.

"So, there'll be no lager on your shopping lists?" joked Clem, with tongue in cheek.

"Absolutely not," replied Alf.

"No chance!" exclaimed Peter.

"Okay, well once you've finished your breakfasts, we can get going," said Clem.

"*Yes, but aren't you forgetting something?*" replied Alf.

"What's that?" asked Clem.

"Our uniforms! We need to change, you pillock!" shrieked Alf, in a panic.

"Oops, yes, I forgot about that," joked Clem.

"We'll be put on a charge, if we got caught outside, in these clothes. I'm sure," said Peter.

"Nope, I don't think it's that serious," replied Clem.

"Well, do you wanna try it, and find out?" asked Peter.

"No thanks, I think I'll pass on that one," replied Clem. Alf and Peter burst into fits of laughter, at that reply.

"Come on then, let's get changed, Peter," stated Alf. "And Clem, we'll meet up with you outside the main gates, in ten minutes," he added.

"Okay chaps!" replied Clem.

The two airmen, Alf and Peter made rapid tracks towards the billet, and Clem waited in the Airmen's Mess. He decided to opt for another cup of tea, and whiled away the time by browsing through the morning newspaper, that he'd just bought from the NAAFI shop outside. It was a mixture of politics, sport and show business gossip, but nothing interested him in particular. There was no news on either Aston Villa or Tottenham Hotspur, and even Hull City and Hull Kingston Rovers were blank for news. But as the saying goes, no news is good news. Although Clem never knew what that actually meant, because if you don't get any news, how do you know if things are good or bad? It was a strange old catch phrase, and one that Clem never truly got his head around.

Clem met up with Alf and Peter, outside the RAF Hereford main gates, as arranged, ten minutes later, and they all hopped on the next bus that had arrived, which was heading for the town centre, as it handily stopped just outside the RAF station. It was convenient and it was packed, all with airmen and airwomen, from the Royal Air Force base.

Clem paid his fare to the female conductor, with her dyed black hair, slicked back, her make up slapped on her face, covering moles and blemishes aplenty, and with her lipstick glossy and bright pink. She must have been all of seventy years old, but she was still going strong, pacing up and down the bus, to take the paying fares from the RAF personnel, that had stayed on the RAF site for the weekend, and there was a fair good number of them too. The bus company must have made a roaring trade from this RAF station alone, never mind from the residents of the housing estates scattered all around the vicinity of RAF Hereford, on the way to the town centre.

Clem settled himself down on the bus, and felt a pair of eyes burning a hole into the back of his head. It was by instinct, that he decided to turn round to see what was causing it. When he glanced over, he was amazed to see the WRAF that was giving him the weird gut feeling, staring straight at him, without the blink of her eye, and he smiled a friendly acknowledgement at her, and she half smiled back, in reply. It excited Clem, and he had a warm, tingly feeling inside. He wasn't sure where this was going, but he was ready to enjoy the journey, nonetheless. Even though the weird gut feeling was playing havoc with his stomach, and giving him a multitude of butterflies. He didn't let on to either Alf nor Peter, and kept it a secret. He didn't want them bustling in and ruining his chances with the WRAF. It was every man for himself, when it came to the opposite sex, even with this one, who gave Clem the creeps. But he knew there was something about her, which he couldn't put his finger on. It was just a matter of finding out, exactly what it was.

Clem didn't turn around again, although he was tempted. But he thought that if he did, he might stir up Alf and Peter's interest, and that would be like shooting himself in the foot. He was maturing rapidly since being in the Royal Air Force, and his experiences at RAF Swinderby and RAF Hereford were teaching him the pure facts of life, on learning how to control his impulsiveness, and taking his time in important matters, *and pulling a hot WRAF at the same time, was definitely in that category.*

The bus trundled on towards the Hereford town centre, and Clem was busy making notes in a small jotter book, for the things that he needed to buy. On top of the list was the Stevie Wonder album, "Songs In The Key Of Life," and this was an album that he was looking forward to listening to. Other items on Clem's shopping list included aftershave, razors, soap, toothpaste and antiperspirant deodorant. He also scribbled down pen and paper, as he was running out of space on his current writing pad, and he knew that his pen would run out of ink very soon too, so he was being prepared for that eventuality. "This list should cover all the things that I need urgently," thought Clem.

The bus arrived at the Hereford town centre, approximately twenty five minutes after leaving the RAF camp. Clem, Alf and Peter joined the queue of people that were waiting to get off the vehicle, and Clem looked for the WRAF woman that gave him the weird gut feeling, but she was nowhere to be seen, and had disappeared into thin air. He shook his head in disbelief, as he was itching to get to talk to her, but he wasn't so sure if she was thinking the same, or if the feeling was mutual, in any way, shape or form. Only time would tell, and Clem used all his recently learned skills in patience, tolerance, diligence and coherence, to the full, in an attempt to remain cool, calm and collected. Alf and Peter hadn't twigged on about him and the WRAF bird, and that was just how Clem wanted it. The three airmen alighted from the bus, and grouped together to discuss their plan of action, on the pavement nearby.

"Where to first, then guys?" asked Clem.

"I'm not bothered where we go," replied Alf, with a shrug of his shoulders.

"Me neither. Anywhere will do me," agreed Peter.

"Okay, let's find a record shop, as I need to buy an LP," stated Clem eagerly.

The other two airmen nodded in agreement, and they all trundled off together, along the wide pathway, towards the Hereford main street, which wasn't too far from the bus station, and where all the shops and stores seemed to be located. It didn't taked Clem long to find the nearest record shop, as it was inside a Woolworths store, and it stocked just about everything under the sun, and was more than just a record shop. Clem discovered that it stocked the aftershave that he needed, and the razors, soap, toothpaste and deodorant too. It was a mega store in its own right, and nothing could beat Woolworths for price, as the cost was very competitive indeed. There was no need to shop around. This place had everything on Clem's shopping list. He was pleased that they stocked the long playing record, "Songs In The Key Of Life," by Stevie Wonder, and he decided to buy a copy in cassette tape form, to play on his trusty old cassette recorder. He was easily pleased, and this purchase made his day. He couldn't wait to get back to the billet to play it.

When Clem's shopping spree ended, with his final two purchases, which were a pen and a pad of writing paper, he was chuffed to bits, and as he waited in the queue to pay for it all, his attention was roused by the WRAF, who gave him the weird gut feeling, and who was standing at the other end of the queue. She glanced at Clem, but didn't crack her face. Clem glanced back, but ignored the impulse to be stony faced, and he smiled cheesily and pleasantly back at her, like a Cheshire Cat. He felt confident, reassured and fearless, as he prepared to introduce himself. There was a shop full of customers, and a few members of the Woolworths staff present, but it didn't bother Clem.

"Hi," he called. "My name's Clem!"

The WRAF didn't reply.

"How's your day going?" called Clem persistently.

"Get lost!" replied the WRAF, who had given Clem the strange gut feeling.

"Eh, what are you on about?" asked Clem.

"I said, get lost, pest!" reiterated the WRAF abruptly, and in no uncertain terms.

Clem shook his head in disbelief. He wasn't sure what he had done wrong, but he didn't pursue the conversation. He merely put it to the back of his mind, and down to experience. Even though he had studied O Level Sociology at A grade, he hadn't a clue about the mind of a woman. And he reckoned if he studied Sociology to degree level, he would never fathom out what makes the female species tick. It wasn't Sociology he needed for this predicament, but Psychology. But Clem had no interest in that subject, only Sociology. Although he knew he would never study it to degree level, he didn't rule out studying Sociology at A Level, one day.

"What's eating you?" asked Alf, in Clem's direction.

"Nothing, why?" replied Clem.

"Because you've gone all mardy, mate," stated Alf, crudely.

"What do you mean?" asked Clem.

"I was trying to talk to you, but you completely ignored me," revealed Alf.

"Oh, sorry mate. I didn't mean to," replied Clem.

"*Have you got more women troubles*?" asked Alf.

"No! Why do you ask?" replied Clem.

"Because I can tell by your attitude, pal," stated Alf.

"Nah, I'm fine!" insisted Clem.

"Are you sure?" asked Alf.

"Yep!" exclaimed Clem, impatiently.

"I reckon it's another bird," said Peter, piping up.

"What makes you say that?" asked Clem.

"I saw you trying it on, with that fat WRAF, over there!" replied Peter.

"*She's not fat*!" snapped Clem, giving the game away.

"Yep, it's true. You're mardy over another woman!" exclaimed Alf.

"I'm not, I'm sure," stated Clem.

"You are. You're all touchy and sensitive about her across there, when I called her fat," said Peter.

"Why don't you ever learn Clem? *Let the birds come to you*!" exclaimed Alf.

Clem didn't reply to that remark. But it was food for thought. Maybe he was trying too hard. But he did have the sense of a weird feeling in his gut, over this WRAF, which wouldn't go away, and the problem was slowly but surely increasing, and becoming clearer for him to see.

"What are you guys buying?" asked Clem, quickly changing the subject.

"Nothing in particular, for me," replied Alf.

"Nor me. I'm just thankful for the fresh air, and the stretch of my legs!" seconded Peter.

"Yes, me too! That study room is rather claustrophobic and stuffy!" exclaimed Alf.

"It sure is, I'm more of an outside sort of fellow, myself," stated Peter.

"Yes, so am I!" agreed Clem.

"That makes three us, then!" exclaimed Alf.

"So, if we all get the same posting, after the trade training, whose applying to work in Petrol Oils and Lubricants?" asked Clem, with tongue in cheek.

"Me!" replied Alf.

"And me, too!" seconded Peter.

"Me, three!" agreed Clem.

"That'll be fun. All three of us applying for POL, at the same RAF base!" stated Alf, with a snigger.

"To be honest, I don't think we'll all be allowed to be posted, to the same base," remarked Clem.

"Maybe not, but you never know," replied Peter.

"Where are you hoping to be posted?" asked Alf, directing his question to Clem.

"I'm not sure. I haven't thought about it, to be honest," replied Clem.

"I have! I'm opting for RAF Marham, RAF Scampton and RAF Wittering," stated Alf.

"Wow, are you? I'm plumping for RAF Brize Norton, RAF Cranwell and RAF Halton," said Peter.

"I haven't got the foggiest. But if push comes to shove, I'll be choosing RAF Finningley, RAF Coltishall and RAF Saint Mawgan, I think," said Clem, choosing the three Royal Air Force bases, from the top of his head.

"Okay, but there's no gaurantee you'll be handed your choice. It all depends if there are vacancies there," informed Alf.

"Yep well, that's pretty obvious, isn't it?" replied Clem.

"I suppose so!" agreed Alf.

"*You watch, we'll all end up being posted to RAF Stafford*!" exclaimed Peter.

"That will be a laugh, but I'm not so sure there's a POL department there!" stated Alf.

"There must be!" replied Clem.

"I thought it was just an RAF stores distribution centre," said Alf.

"It is!" exclaimed Peter.

"*So, there's no Petrol Oils and Lubricants*?" asked Alf.

"It's not an active operational RAF base, as such, so there'll be no Liquid Oxygen or aviation fuel issued. But I'm sure there's other POL stuff," said Clem.

"Only time will tell, eh?" replied Alf.

The three airmen left the Woolworths store, and walked around the Hereford town centre, browsing, window shopping and killing time, in a relaxed and easy going manner. They had nothing else to do, and the weather was fine for late November, so they couldn't grumble. But nobody bought anything else, from any of the stores or shops.

They stopped off at a cafe and ordered tea and buns. Clem chose a sticky chocolate coated donut, which he devoured in next to no time. He also munched a ham sandwich and a Mars Bar, as he was absolutely famished. Nothing much was spoken by the three lads. They just drank their hot tea and consumed their food, before heading to the bus station, to make their way back to the RAF Hereford base camp.

"What's it going to be tonight, then lads?" asked Clem, as they approached a large Debenhams department store, on the way to the bus station.

"I don't know. Television again, maybe?" replied Alf.

"Yep. Television is a good idea!" agreed Peter.

"Okay. Television it is!" stated Clem, with a nod of his head. "Let's take a look in here, as the football results will be on!" he added, making a detour through the Debenhams store, towards the television department.

"Oh yes, the games should be just about over by now. It's nearly a quarter to five!" replied Alf excitedly.

"I wanna see if my teams have won," said Clem.

"Who's your teams?" asked Alf.

"Tottenham Hotspur, Aston Villa and Hull City," replied Clem.

"Bloody hell, *you've got three of them*?" asked Alf.

"Yep, Hull City are my home town team, where I come from, and Villa and Spurs are just pure class! I've supported Spurs since the sixties, and Villa for around a year," explained Clem.

"Oh, right, I see," replied Alf.

"I kept a budgie once, and called it Cyril, after the Tottenham Hotspur player, Cyril Knowles!" exclaimed Clem, looking at Peter "Squeaky" Bird, for a reaction. "Do you know "Nice One Cyril," the Spurs footie song?"

"Yes, I remember it. *Did you really keep a budgie?*" asked Peter.

"Yep, it was white for Tottenham Hotspur, and I was about fourteen years old at the time. But I really treasured that bird! I cleaned it out, fed and watered it, the lot!" exclaimed Clem proudly.

"So you should, if it was your pet, mate. I'm not being funny, but that's what owners do!" replied Alf, with tongue in cheek.

"Yep, that's true. I was a good owner," agreed Clem.

"*A white budgie?*" asked Peter.

"Yes, it was mainly white, with a patch of blue on its chest, in accordance with the Tottenham Hotspur team colours!" exclaimed Clem.

"Wow, it sounds like you're really keen on Spurs!" replied Peter.

"Yes I am, but they're struggling at the minute, and might be in danger of relegation, hence my support for Aston Villa, who are on the up and up. So they're covering for Spurs, whilst they're going through a bit of a rough patch," explained Clem.

"Oh, I see," replied Peter.

"What teams do you support?" asked Clem, directing his question to both Alf and Peter.

"Nobody really," lied Alf in embarrassment, hiding his team's identity, who were Doncaster Rovers.

"Stoke City," replied Peter.

"Okay, fine," said Clem.

The airmen reached the Debenhams store television department, and spotted a large gathering of males, and some females too, huddling around the television screens, that were tuned in to the football results, on both the ITV and BBC 1 channels. Clem, Alf and Peter dashed quickly over, to check on their teams outcome.

"Coventry City 1 Aston Villa 1," called out the score caster.

"Tottenham Hotspur 2 Stoke City 0," stated the score caster, a few seconds later.

"Bristol Rovers 3 Hull City 0," said the score caster, a few minutes after that.

"Wow, Tottenham played Stoke today!" exclaimed Clem.

"Yep, so I see," replied Peter, shrugging his shoulders in disappointment.

"And Spurs won two-nil! Yippee!" shrieked Clem, with thrilling excitement in his tone. "Against your lot, Peter!"

"Yep, so I heard!" moaned Peter.

"*But Hull City were thrashed, three-nil*!" piped up Alf, bursting Clem's bubble.

"Yep, they were, by Bristol Rovers," agreed Clem, with a frown.

"And Aston Villa drew one-one with Coventry away," said Alf, craftily checking on Doncaster Rovers three-nil win against Crewe, but still keeping quiet about them.

"A mixed set of results for me then. Spurs win, Villa draw and Hull City lose," reflected Clem philosophically.

"That's what you call a full house!" chirped Alf, with positivity shining through, in his tone.

"Yep, which is a great deal better than my lot managed. Which was a loss!" exclaimed Peter.

"Yes, that's surprised me. As Spurs are looking like certain candidates for relegation, even though we are not even half way through the season yet. But a win today against Stoke was a definite shock," revealed Clem, with honesty.

"Yes, I agree. It certainly shocked me. As I was expecting at least a score draw, if not better. But I didn't expect a defeat," replied Peter.

"Never mind, there's always the next game!" exclaimed Clem.

"That's true. But you're only as good as your last match. Which means Spurs are pretty good, Stoke are crap, Hull are worse, and Aston Villa are just so-so," joked Peter.

"I agree. But it's only disguising Spurs awful form though, as they aren't that good at the moment," commented Clem.

"*Do you really think they'll get relegated*?" asked Alf.

"Yes I do. There's no way they'll stay up!" replied Clem.

"Bloody hell! That's a strong opinion, so early in the season. It's not even Christmas yet!" exclaimed Alf.

"So what! I can feel it in my bones, and to tell you the truth, this season can't end quickly enough for me. So Spurs can regroup and rebuild next season in the Second Division, as it's all that they deserve," stated Clem, with honesty.

"Have faith mate, they might pull it around," enthused Alf.

"Nope, I doubt it. It's been coming for years. They're a tired old team, full of players on the verge of retirement, that haven't been replaced. It's a shame. But that's how it goes. I'm sure they'll come back stronger in the future. But not this year!" replied Clem, with strong passion.

"Nah, I beg to differ. I think they'll survive this season, and fight tooth and nail to stay up," stated Alf.

"If I was a betting man, I'd put a wager on it with you, but I'm not!" exclaimed Clem.

"Go on! I bet you a tenner, that Spurs stay up," replied Alf.

"Okay, you're on!" exclaimed Clem, shaking hands with Alf on the £10 bet, to confirm it.

"Brilliant! But I hope you don't mind parting with a tenner, though!" replied Alf, with tongue in cheek.

"You've got to be joking!" shrieked Clem.

"You're nearly right, but I'm Alf King, not Joe King! *Joe's my middle name*!" replied Alf facetiously, with a cheeky chortle.

"Yes, very funny!" stated Clem, with a half a smile of disgust, at the Mickey take.

"Wow! That's what the vicar said, at my christening!" joked Alf.

"I'm not surprised," answered Clem. "It's not everyday that you meet someone called Joe King!" he added.

"He thought it was a joke too, until my mother insisted vehemently that it wasn't," stressed Alf.

"Did she really?" asked Clem.

"Yes, and you don't want to see my mother, when she's insisting vehemently, as it's not a pretty sight," stated Alf, with a straight face.

"*Are you still taking the Mickey*?" asked Clem.

"I'll let you make up your own mind, on that one!" exclaimed Alf.

Clem frowned and couldn't decide on whether Alf was pulling his leg or not, but he decided to go with the flow, giving Alf the benefit of the doubt. He decided there and then, quickly and decisively, that he would not like to meet Alf's mother, when she was being "*vehemently insistent.*"

The three airmen left Debenhams, and caught a bus back to the RAF Hereford training base. It was a slow and meandering journey, that stopped at every bus stop, and the double decker vehicle was packed, smoky and uncomfortable. Clem hadn't felt this bad since travelling back from Flamingo Park, when he was in the Cub Scouts, aged seven or eight, and was sat on a coach, next to the window, and suffered sunstroke. His head ached so much that day, that he thought it was going to explode. He had hated travelling on buses ever since, and that was ten years ago. He just wanted to get off this bus, and walk back the rest of the way. At least he would have some fresh air in his lungs. But he decided against that drastic action, and persevered with the awful conditions, with a grimace and a stiff upper lip.

As soon as the three airmen arrived back at the RAF Hereford base, they headed straight to the Airmen's Mess. They were famished again, and seemed to be at the age of being constantly hungry, and whether this was a growing spurt, or just plain old greediness, nobody could decide. But nevertheless, there was no doubt about it, they ate like starving gannets.

"So, about the television tonight, then. Is there anything on?" asked Clem looking at both Alf and Peter, for an answer.

"I'm not sure. Match Of The Day, at ten o'clock, I know for a fact will be on. But other than that, I'm not certain," replied Alf.

"I think there's a film on at eight o'clock, on BBC One, whilst ITV have the Bionic Woman," replied Peter.

"Oh, interesting. I wonder what film it is?" asked Clem.

"I don't know. But the Generation Game is on around seven o'clock, on BBC One, also," stated Peter, proving he was a fountain of knowledge, on the Saturday night television programmes.

"Yes, I think I've seen that," agreed Clem.

"The Sale of the Century is on too, I think, on ITV," replied Peter, being extra helpful.

"*It's all quiz and game shows*!" exclaimed Clem, in disbelief.

"Yep, that's what makes us English competitive. We all like a good game show to watch!" replied Alf, piping up.

"Are Morcambe and Wise on?" asked Clem.

"Yes, I think they're on BBC One, after the film," replied Peter.

"That'll be worth a watch! They're quite funny!" exclaimed Clem.

"Yes, they are," agreed Alf and Peter, together in unison.

"Oh well, it sounds like there's a fair few decent programmes to watch, before Match Of The Day, when Spurs will be on, following their fine two-nil demolition of Stoke City!" exclaimed Clem.

"Yes, don't remind me! I think I'll go back to the billet, when that comes on!" replied Peter, with tongue in cheek.

"Really?" asked Clem facetiously.

"Yes, I can't stand watching my team get beat. It doesn't make good viewing!" confirmed Peter.

"You can say that again! I know all about that feeling!" replied Clem.

Clem got back to his room, after the Saturday night television session, and had to admit to himself, that the highlight of the night, was the Tottenham Hotspur v Stoke City football game, on Match Of The Day, by a long chalk. The other programmes weren't too bad, but nothing was going to take away the joy of seeing Spurs record a famous win, after so many disappointing results recently. Morcambe and Wise didn't let him down either, and provided Clem with a good laugh. The feature film on BBC 1, was the old John Wayne western, "True Grit," and Clem couldn't remember anything about it. He thought he must have fallen asleep for the majority of the time it was on. Apart from these couple of programmes, *Match Of The Day* and *The Morcambe and Wise Show*, Clem couldn't really say much about the others. But it couldn't take away the happiness he felt, after seeing Spurs stun Stoke. He slept like a top, and woke up the next morning, feeling refreshed, renewed and full of vigour. It was Sunday!

Clem hadn't the foggiest idea what he was going to do today, but he wasn't too concerned about that. He was determined to make the most of enjoying a last hurrah Sunday, before getting back to the strict supply trade training regime, in the morning.

Breakfast was good again. Then a flick through the Sunday morning newspapers for Clem, especially the sports pages, with the Tottenham Hotspur match report being a priority. But there was still no sign of Alf or Peter, although Clem didn't dismay. He went back to his billet, stretched out on his bed, and relaxed at full tilt, until lunch time.

Clem enjoyed reading the match report, regarding Tottenham Hotspur's 2-0 win over Stoke City so much, that he read it five times in a row, just in case he missed something. It had been ages, since Clem had been given an opportunity to read a match report, that was so glowing and positive about Spurs, because the last few results were a 2-1 loss away to Sunderland, last week, a 1-0 home defeat against Bristol City, the week before that, then a 5-3 hammering at West Ham, a 3-3 draw at home to Everton, a 1-0 defeat at home to Coventry, an 8-2 thumping away to Derby County, and a 4-2 mauling at West Bromwich Albion.

They did manage a 1-0 win at home to Birmingham City, in the middle of all those terrible results, but that was six weeks ago. Two wins and a draw, in nine matches wasn't exactly great form, and in those matches, it saw Spurs concede twenty four goals in all, and only scoring fourteen in reply, which was a deficit of ten, and thirteen points had been dropped. Unlucky for some, and definitely unlucky for Tottenham Hotspur. It was easy to see why Clem was worried about relegation. When your team gets beaten 4-2, you expect a positive reaction. But when that reaction doesn't materialise, and an 8-2 defeat follows closely after, only two weeks later, followed by a 5-3 thrashing, three weeks after that, then things are beginning to look ominous, and Clem knew his £10 bet, was as safe as houses. There were some ugly scorelines among those results, and that had only been from the 2nd October, a few days before Clem had joined up for the RAF. In eight weeks, Tottenham Hotspur had picked up only five points from a possible eighteen, including the result against Stoke City yesterday. So Clem made the most of this latest winning result, and hoped the tide was turning. But he wasn't going to hold his breath, in any way, shape or form.

Clem went for lunch, with the sobering thought of Tottenham Hotspur having lost six games in the last nine, nestled in his head. But as Alf had already pointed out to him, your team is only as good as the last result, and having won that one, 2-0, Clem clutched hard to that upbeat thought, to keep himself positive, and worked hard at trying to forget the 8-2 mauling at Derby County, the 5-3 hammering at West Ham, and the 4-2 slaughter at West Bromwich Albion. Instead he filled up his mind with the thoughts of yesterday's 2-0 win against Stoke City, with the newspaper report he had just read, as well as last night's action on Match Of The Day, assisting him in his quest.

Clem bumped into Alf and Peter in the Airmen's Mess, and he joined them at their table. The room was full of diners, and Clem wondered if anyone had bothered to go home for the weekend, as the place was just as full as it had been during the week.

"What are you up to?" asked Clem.

"Nothing much, what about you?" replied Alf.

"Sunday papers, and that's about it," answered Clem.

"*Sundays are boring! Always have been, always will be!*" complained Alf, in no uncertain terms.

"Yes, but they are supposed to be, as it's a day of rest," replied Clem, passionately.

"Still boring though!" reiterated Alf.

"What have you got planned, for this afternoon?" asked Clem.

"I wanted to play badminton, but Peter here doesn't want to lark," replied Alf.

"Don't worry, I'll play!" said Clem keenly.

"Really, have you played badminton before?" asked Alf.

"Yep, many years ago, in junior school," replied Clem.

"Are you any good?" asked Alf.

"I dunno. I haven't played, since I was about twelve," replied Clem.

"Okay, you'll do as a playing partner, as I'm not all that good myself. So it'll be a fair match," answered Alf.

"Okay, you're on!" replied Clem.

"Great, let's go then!" exclaimed Alf.

"*What about me?*" moaned Peter.

"You said you didn't want to play!" replied Alf, pointing out his accusation clearly, with a tone of annoyance in his voice.

"*I know, but I've changed my mind*," stated Peter.

"It's too late, mate! You've missed out. But you can watch if you like, or be the scorer for us," suggested Alf.

"Nah, it's okay. I think I'll give that a miss, thanks all the same," replied Peter.

"Why, it'll be something to do," encouraged Alf.

"Nope. It'll be like watching paint dry," joked Peter, with tongue in cheek.

"Oh okay, fine. If you say so," replied Alf, turning round to make his way outside. "Come on Clem, let's go!"

Clem and Alf swiftly made their way outside, and left Peter cutting a forlorn figure, at the dining table.

"Will Peter be okay?" asked Clem, as they left the Airman's Mess.

"Yes, I reckon he'll be fine. He did after all, have first refusal to play, but blew his chance, so that's his problem," replied Alf, cruelly.

There was music playing in the Airman's Mess, as the two airmen left. It was "Money Money Money" by Abba, and Clem reckoned this track seemed to be playing non stop. But it was okay, as Clem liked the song. It was catchy, funky and upbeat, and it was music at its best, thought Clem.

The two airmen made their way inside the sports hall, after a short journey by foot, and lo and behold, there was music playing inside there too, and Clem was amazed to hear Abba again, singing "Money Money Money." He laughed quietly to himself, and wasn't sure if it was the same piped music from the Airman's Mess, or from a completely different media. But it tickled him, and it raised his spirits tenfold.

"Okay, we're here. Now we need to go to the reception desk, to hire rackets and a court," stated Alf.

"Right, let's do it!" replied Clem.

Clem and Alf booked an hour, and reckoned that would be ample time to exhaust themselves.

They were handed a racket each and a shuttlecock, which was a small round half ping pong ball, with a circular feather lodged around it, shaped in a cone. There was no charge. It was all free and that made a welcome change for Clem, as he often had to pay £1.50 for an hour of hard court tennis, with his brother, when he played on the Hull city council owned land at East Park, before he joined the RAF.

More music started, that played all around the large spacious sports hall, and it was Dana, with her hit record "Fairytale," bellowing loudly and brightly to the sporting fanatics of the Royal Air Force, who were all busy playing badminton, and other pursuits. There were half a dozen badminton courts, six table tennis tables, half a dozen snooker tables, six pool tables, a cafe, a vending machine and a ladies and gents toilet facility, all squeezed into this massive sporting complex, and the whole place was heaving. There was noise, atmosphere, banter, screaming, joy, happiness and effort, all going on in there, and everyone seemed to be having a whale of a time. Clem couldn't wait to get started. He was in the mood to play a decent game, and with his natural winning mentality, he was hoping to win. Even if it was just for the bragging rights. As he was in a very determined mood, this afternoon.

The game began in earnest, and both players struggled to find a decent rhythm. It was going to take a long while before they warmed up and found their feet. The match was riddled with mistakes, stoppages and delays, as both players got to grips with playing the wonderful game of badminton once again. It was all about timing. Then something clicked and it was nothing to do with the game of badminton, but it was Clem's ankle. He had jumped up to hit a hard shot over the net, and as he landed on the ground, he turned his ankle awkwardly, and felt an immediate surging pain, shooting down his leg, from his calf, to his Achilles tendon.

"Arrgghhhh!" yelled Clem, in agony.

"What's up?" called Alf.

"My ankle!" screamed Clem.

"Okay! Okay! Don't move! Stay perfectly still!" ordered Alf.

"*Where are you going?*" asked Clem, as he glanced across to watch Alf disappear out of view.

"I'm going for the First Aid box!" Alf replied, urgently.

Clem lay on the ground holding his damaged ankle, and he couldn't move, even if he wanted to. Alf returned a few minutes later, armed with a First Aid box, some bandages and a jar of cold water.

"*Where did you get all that from?*" asked Clem.

"Over there in the cafe. And watch out, the water might be freezing, as there are ice cubes in it," warned Alf.

"Okay," replied Clem, preparing himself for the cold, harsh shock, as Alf hovered with the jar of the freezing cold water, above Clem's ankle.

"Are you ready?" asked Alf, as he prepared to administer the water.

"Yep, go ahead!" replied Clem. "Arrgghhh! Wow, that's cold!" Clem added, screaming his head off.

"I did warn you," stated Alf.

"Ohhhhh, it was worse than I thought it would be," replied Clem.

"Give over, you big baby! *This will do you the power of good*!" exclaimed Alf.

"Why, how do you know it will? Have you been on a First Aid course?" asked Clem.

"Yes I have, as a matter of fact, for the Saint John Ambulance. So don't worry, you're in good hands," replied Alf.

"Okay, I'll trust you," said Clem.

"It looks like you've badly sprained it. So badminton will be out of the question for a couple of weeks," explained Alf. "*At least!*" he added.

Clem's injury was worse than he first feared. The ice cold water helped to bring out the extent of the strain, but the pain was still horrific, and Clem struggled to put any weight on the injured ankle, however minute. It was the worst pain he had ever suffered in all his seventeen years, and he knew he needed more than just an ice pack and crepe bandage for it.

"I'm gonna need a medic for this!" stressed Clem, with pain evident on his face.

"Nah, it's not that serious! You'll be alright after a couple of paracetamol," advised Alf.

"Nope, I don't agree! I'm off to report myself sick!" replied Clem.

"Don't be so daft!" answered Alf. "You'll end up being back-flighted!" he added.

"I don't care, I'm in absolute agony here!" replied Clem with a heartfelt passion in his tone. "And I can't go on like this! It's impossible to move!" he added, with a very serious face.

Clem struggled to his feet, and looked awkward in his stance, like he was about to collapse in a heap.

"*Well, are you going to help me get to the Medical Centre?*" asked Clem in a threatening tone. "*Or not?*" he added.

"I suppose so, if you insist," replied Alf, taking Clem by the arm and supporting him on the left hand side, where Clem's injured ankle was providing him with great discomfort. "I'm serious about you getting back-flighted, if you miss any of the training course," Alf insisted.

"That's rubbish! It's not that I've gone AWOL, or been arrested by the RAF police. I'm injured, but I can still study, laid up in hospital," replied Clem.

"You won't be admitted into hospital. You'll be packed off back to the billet, with a few painkillers, and told to rest up. I bet you!" exclaimed Alf.

"Nah, I don't wanna bet, and take any more money off you. I've already got the Spurs ten pounds relegation bet won!" replied Clem, with tongue in cheek.

Clem presented himself to the RAF Hereford Medical Centre, and was seen by the duty medic almost immediately. There were no long queues, delays or excuses. The duty medic was clinical, efficient and knowledgeable about the type of injury Clem had suffered.

"*You've a badly sprained ankle there, mate,*" stated the male duty medic, who was an SAC rank, with short blond hair, a chubby face and a distinctive dimple in his chin, making him resemble a young Kirk Douglas.

"Okay fine, I gathered that!" replied Clem impatiently, which was unlike his normal attitude. But he was in agony, and hadn't the tolerance for obvious statements of prognosis.

"We shall have to monitor you for approximately twenty four hours. So we'll be keeping you in here, on the ward until the morning, to see if the swelling has subsided," said the Kirl Douglas look-alike.

"Okay, fine," replied Clem, looking across at Alf with an expression of "told you so," written across his face.

Clem was right about being kept in, and he regretted not taking Alf up on the bet, as he would have been ten quid richer, but he didn't fret about it. Alf glanced back at Clem with a look of relief on his face, as if to say he was pleased he hadn't shook on the wager, as he would have been *ten quid poorer.*

"Are you on a training course, here at RAF Hereford?" asked the Kirk Douglas look-alike.

"Yep," replied Clem.

"Which one?" asked the Kirk Douglas look-alike.

"Supply," replied Clem.

"Okay, we shall contact their admin team in the morning, if you are kept in here for longer than twenty four hours, and let them know of your whereabouts," explained the Kirk Douglas look-alike.

"Thank you," replied Clem, looking forward to having some time off.

The Kirk Douglas look-alike filled out an official RAF medical form, on Clem's behalf, asked some more questions, and Clem provided the answers. Alf left the Medical Centre soon after, and returned to the billet block, leaving Clem to settle down on the ward, to rest and recuperate, after being given pain killers.

Next morning, when Clem woke up, he had to admit to himself that he had a bit of an unsettled sort of night on the ward, as he reckoned his Medical Centre bed was lumpy, bumpy and uncomfortable. He grumbled and moaned to himself, but he didn't let on to the female duty medic, when she came in to check on his condition, for fear of being branded a miserable beggar.

"Good morning!" sang the female duty medic, as bright as a new button, and who was a dark brown haired, dark brown eyed SACW, with a chunky pair of legs, that made her look like an athlete of some kind, and Clem was guessing that she was either a hammer thrower, javelin thrower or a shot putter. She certainly looked fit, in Clem's estimation and was sociable, friendly and approachable too.

"Good morning!" replied Clem, sitting up in his lumpy, bumpy bed and unable to take his eyes off her gorgeous legs.

"How are you today?" asked the chunky-legged SACW medic.

"I'm fine, thanks," lied Clem.

"Good, good. How's the ankle?" asked the chunky-legged SACW medic.

"It's not so bad, thanks. The pain's just about gone," replied Clem cheerfully.

"Excellent. Let's have a look then," demanded the chunky-legged SACW medic, forcefully.

"Okay," replied Clem, throwing the bed sheet and blankets to one side, to reveal his injured ankle, and fortunately for the chunky-legged female medic, Clem had remembered to keep his boxer shorts on, to stop any embarrassing moments.

"Yes, it looks like it's reduced in swelling, compared to last night," stated the chunky-legged SACW medic. "After I had popped in, to have a look, at the start of my night shift, when you were asleep," she added.

"*Awwww, does that mean I've got to return to normal training duties?*" asked Clem.

"Yes, it looks like it," replied the chunky-legged SACW medic.

"Oh no, I was looking forward to a few days holiday!" sighed Clem in agony. "I mean recuperation," he quickly followed up, to correct his previous statement, in case he was accused of desertion of duty.

"Never mind, eh! You must be a quick healer!" exclaimed the chunky-legged SACW medic, with a smile.

"Yep, sure. Maybe I am!" exclaimed Clem. "By the way. Do you mind if I ask you a personal question?" he requested.

"Of course not, go ahead," replied the SACW with the chunky legs.

"Are you the sporty type?" asked Clem bravely, and as clear as a bell.

"*Me? Whatever made you think that?*" replied the chunky-legged SACW medic, with a giggle.

"I was just wondering, that's all," stated Clem, coolly, calmly and collectedly.

"As a matter of fact, I am, actually," revealed the chunky-legged SACW medic.

"Oh, really, wow! That's amazing!" replied Clem, fixing his stare on her shapely and muscular chunky legs.

"Yep, I play netball, hockey, tennis and volleyball, for the Royal Air Force," stated the chunky-legged SACW medic.

"Do you really? Is that for RAF Hereford?" asked Clem.

"No, not RAF Hereford. But the actual Royal Air Force national team!" explained the chunky-legged SACW medic.

"Wow, brilliant! I could tell that, by the way you look. You seem fit and strong!" exclaimed Clem.

"Thank you, I'm very flattered!" replied the chunky-legged SACW medic.

"That's alright, it's my pleasure," stated Clem confidently. The chunky-legged SACW medic blushed as she made her way out of the room, and Clem couldn't keep his eyes off her amazing legs, as she walked away.

Clem had breakfast in the Medical Centre, and was then discharged. He returned to his billet room to shave, and to change into his RAF uniform. It was ten past eight, and training didn't start until nine, so he had plenty of time. His ankle was holding up well, and he was pleased he had suffered no adverse setbacks to the injury, although it had been well strapped up by the chunky-legged SACW medic. As Clem was busy getting ready for the day ahead, he bumped into Stuart Saunders, the Swindon Town supporter, that was bunked up in the next bed to him, in the billet.

"How's it going?" asked Clem.

"Not bad, thanks. How's you?" replied Stuart, looking at Clem like he had seen a ghost.

"Fine, except I've just spent the night in the Medical Centre, after badly spraining my ankle, playing badminton," revealed Clem, with a chortle.

"Oh no! I wondered where you had got to, after seeing your bed unoccupied all night! How is it?" asked Stuart.

"A lot better than yesterday, thank you," replied Clem.

"Good, good. Did you hear about Brad, the steward from Hull?" asked Stuart.

"No, what about him?" replied Clem, with intrigue in his tone.

"He was killed in a car crash, in Derby, last night," answered Stuart.

"No!" replied Clem, in a dramatic tone of voice. "What happened?" he added, in deep shock.

"I dunno. I heard about it from another steward, on his course, as Brad was pretty well known and popular with everyone, and he knew him from RAF Swinderby too," explained Stuart.

"Well, I can't believe it. As I was asked by Brad if I was interested in travelling back to Hull, for the weekend. But after a little thought, I declined the offer, as I wanted to sample the RAF Hereford weekend life, *and also the*

WRAFs," stated Clem, slowly and methodically, as he came to terms with the sad news.

"That's what I thought! Someone said you'd gone back to Hull with Brad, and was in the car with him, when it crashed, overturned and caught fire, and when I saw your bed hadn't been slept in all night, I feared the worst!" remarked Stuart dramatically.

"Wow, did all that happen? No, I nearly went, but something stopped me, and I decided to stay here," replied Clem.

"Well, you've been very lucky, mate," remarked Stuart.

"Yes I have. Apart from injuring my ankle, that is," scoffed Clem, with tongue in cheek. "*Playing bloody badminton!*"

"That's fairly minor, compared to what happened to Brad," replied Stuart.

"Yes it is. I was only being facetious," admitted Clem, again with tongue in cheek.

"Have some respect man! An RAF colleague has just lost his life in a car crash. This is not the time to be flippant!" bellowed Stuart.

"True, true. I can't argue with that. I'm sorry, I was out of order," said Clem in reply.

"Anyway, I'm sure we'll hear all about it, in due course. But for now, we've got to carry on with our normal duties, and act as if nothing has happened," stated Stuart positively, but with a long, sad face.

"Yes. Brad seemed a top bloke. Full of energy and spark, and he'll be sadly missed," replied Clem, with a heartfelt emotion, in his tone.

"He sure will, although I didn't know him personally, he was still a member of the RAF family, and that is all that matters," saluted Stuart.

"Here, here. Well said, I fully agree," stated Clem.

Clem finished getting ready for work, or training or whatever it was called here at RAF Hereford. He didn't know anymore, about anything. His head had been well and truly shook up, stirred and whisked around, in a whirlpool of confusion, after the news about Brad, the steward.

It wasn't just his death that had shocked Clem and shaken him up, but it was the fact that he could easily have been in that vehicle, and quite possibly be dead too.

He tried to get his head around the reasoning of what made him stay at the RAF base, when he had an opportunity to go home for the weekend. But the harder he tried to work it out, the tougher it became to make any sense of it all.

His head was in bits and pieces. He knew he was a lucky fellow to be still alive. But he couldn't for the life of him fathom out what made him stay at RAF Hereford. Then he had a brainwave. It was the WRAFs. That was it. *It was the WRAFs, that made him stay at the RAF station.*

Clem studied hard all day, concentrated fully on the training, and reckoned he did well, considering the news he had received at the beginning of the morning, that had got him off to such a bad start. But he put it all to the back of his mind, and plodded on, regardless.

That same night, was the evening of the big match in Scotland, Aberdeen versus Rangers. "Slap Happy" Luke Jappy's team, against Daniel MacJames favourites. The Aberdonian taking on the Glaswegian. And the two Scots let everyone know about it, singing the national anthem of Scotland, with gusto.

"O Flower of Scotland
When will we see your like again
That fought and died for
Your wee bit hill and glen
And stood against him
Proud Edward's army
And sent him homeward
Tae think again
The hills are bare now
And autumn leaves lie thick and still
O'er land that is lost now
Which those so dearly held
And stood against him
Proud Edward's army
And sent him homeward
Tae think again
Those days are passed now
And in the past they must remain
But we can still rise now
And be the nation again
That stood against him
Proud Edward's army

And sent him homeward
Tae think again."

The anthem echoed around the NAAFI bar, as all the Scots in the building rallied round to sing their beloved song, led by Luke Jappy and Daniel MacJames.

The congregation of the Scots split into two groups, one supporting Aberdeen and the other Rangers, and the match was being transmitted live on BBC Radio Two, as it was an important fixture for both clubs, and had grabbed the attention of every Scottish football supporter, including those currently working in England, such as Luke Jappy and Daniel MacJames, and everyone huddled around the radio, in the corner of the NAAFI bar.

Beer flowed, drinks were spilled, banter began, and the rivalry deepened.

The game got underway and Rangers attacked from the beginning, as they went for the jugular. The Rangers manager, Jock Wallace had created an excellent team ethic into his squad, and they played with style, expression and verve, fearing nobody on their travels, and the twenty two thousand spectators, including ten thousand from Rangers, that had crammed into Pittodrie, and had nearly doubled Aberdeen's average attendance, that was normally only around eleven or twelve thousand, made a deafening roar of approval, as the whistle blew to begin the game.

Rangers took an early lead, through Miller, in the 5th minute, and MacDonald added a second, five minutes after that. The Rangers supporters in the NAAFI bar were going bonkers, as were the supporters behind the goal, at Aberdeen's small and compact stadium, which could be heard loud and clear, through the radio. But the Aberdeen fans were hushed into silence.

Aberdeen tightened up their lax defence, and began to play some neat, attractive football, as they were quickly coming to terms with the two early setbacks, *namely the conceding of the two early goals,* and they began to fight back, with a great goal from Jarvie, Aberdeen's top scorer.

The Aberdeen manager, Ally MacLeod had put a lot of faith in this striker, knowing he would come up with the goods, sooner or later, and he wasn't disappointed.

Aberdeen battled relentlessly, to try and secure the equaliser before half time, but Rangers hung on, and defended bravely and stubbornly, with some dour and desperate defence, in the latter stages of the first half, and the Rangers fans were singing loudly and proudly in the stadium, and in the NAAFI bar at RAF Hereford, especially Daniel MacJames, the massive Rangers fan.

But Luke Jappy wasn't too concerned, as football was a game of two halves, and "Slap Happy" Jappy knew his team could mount a comeback, in the next 45 minutes.

Aberdeen came out in the second half, with all their guns blazing, and they attacked Rangers, from all angles. Down the middle, on the flanks, and just about everywhere, playing some bright, entertaining football, to try and secure an equaliser. They were knocking hard at the door, and eventually Scott made the breakthrough, with a fine header, to make the score 2-2. The Aberdeen fans went crazy at Pittodrie, and celebrated just as mad, in the NAAFI bar.

"It's two-two!" teased Luke Jappy in Daniel MacJames face, in a wild celebration. "*It's two-two!*" he repeated, facetiously, dancing around in a circle.

"Yes, okay, okay. It was two-nil a few minutes ago, to Rangers!" replied Daniel MacJames. "So don't count your chickens, just yet!" he added.

Then Aberdeen scored again, through Smith, and the Pittodrie stadium went barmy. Everyone cheered, sang and danced in the ground, *except the ten thousand Rangers fans*, with half of the Scots, supporting Aberdeen in the NAAFI bar also jumping up and down, with joy and elation, in witnessing a dramatic comeback by Aberdeen, from two goals down, to 3-2 up, and the other half, being the Rangers fans, looking sorrowful, sad and sullen. It was what made football such a roller coaster and emotional sporting event.

Jock Wallace was livid with his Rangers defence, and was having a right go at the Rangers goalkeeper Kennedy, and blaming him for the sloppy goals that they had conceded.

Ally MacLeod meanwhile, was jubilant with the transformation, and knew his team could do it.

The Aberdonians were celebrating a victory, until the last few seconds of the match, when a corner came over, and somehow Johnstone of Rangers managed to squeeze the ball over the Aberdeen line, to make the score 3-3. Then a second or two later, the whistle for full time was blown, by the referee.

Daniel MacJames treated the equaliser like it was a winner. After leading 2-0, then being pegged back to 2-2, before going 3-2 down, then equalising in the latter seconds of the game, was just as good as winning, reckoned Daniel. He bounced up and down like a Jack in the box, along with the other hordes of Rangers fans in the NAAFI bar, as they listened to the game live on the NAAFI radio set. It had been a tremendous game of football and something that would stay with Daniel for the rest of his life, and Luke Jappy would not forget this match in a hurry, either. Although he was disappointed with the final result of 3-3, as it felt like a defeat, Luke had seen a spirited fightback from his team, and it showed they had grit and determination ingrained in their back bone.

Coming from two goals down to be actually 3-2 in front, took a lot of character to execute, and Luke was pleased with that aspect of the game, and happy that Aberdeen didn't turn over and die. But conceding a goal at the very end of the match was extremely disappointing to see, and Luke Jappy was gutted that two points were dropped in that manner. However one point was better than none, and after going down 2-0 in the first ten minutes, *that one point looked a million miles away*.

All in all, 3-3 was a fair result thought Clem, as a neutral listener, as he had no association with either of the teams, but listening from the back of the crowd, he could safely say a draw was the perfect outcome, as both sides earned it, and nobody deserved to lose.

The alcohol flowed freely, the banter was raised another notch, and the anthem "Flower of Scotland" piped up again, as both the Rangers and Aberdeen fans celebrated the thrilling 3-3 draw in style, in the only way the Scottish knew how, by consuming plenty of whisky, and raising their glasses to a fantastic football match.

Clem slept better than he thought he would, as the noise was deafening in the billet block, as the Aberdeen and Rangers fans continued their drunken celebrations, with no apparent ending in sight. Clem wondered where they had got all their energy from. And also how they managed to drink so much, without the fear of a hangover in the morning. It must have been all that fresh air on the hills of Bonnie Scotland, or an upbringing of booze from an early age, that it was water off a duck's back, when it came to the recovery time, thought Clem. Eventually at 2am, the noise subsided, and things settled down, and Clem was wondering what would have happened if one of those two teams had actually won the match.

Next day, in class, Clem was there, bright eyed and bushy tailed as normal at 9am, and he was dumbfounded to see Luke Jappy and Daniel MacJames waiting outside the classroom before him, looking fresh faced and as sober as two judges. How on earth did they do it? he wondered. Anyway, he wasn't going to fret about it, as it was far too much, for such an early time of the day, to worry about.

"Okay class, it's time to place your choices of posting on to paper. You shall have three options and one of those, not necessarily the first or second choices, will be your allotted posting. *It might not even be your third preference*, but by providing us with your choices, it shall give the RAF admin team something to work with. So, take your time, have a good think, but not too hard though, eh, "Slap Happy" Jappy, just in case your brain boils over!" quipped Corporal McCauley, with tongue in cheek.

Clem didn't have to think, for long. He chose three instantly, RAF Finningley, RAF Coltishall and RAF St Mawgan, without any hesitation, and handed the paper over to the corporal.

Clem hoped to have his first choice of RAF Finningley approved, as it wasn't too far from Hull, and was easy to travel to, and from. Maybe not on a daily commute, but a weekend jaunt wouldn't be out of the question, every now and again, and maybe it would give Clem a chance to have a break from the washing and ironing of his own clothes, like he had to do at RAF Swinderby and RAF Hereford. Although he would loathe to burden his mother with the hassle of washing and ironing his clobber, on a regular basis. It would be plain unfair to her, thought Clem.

Clem forgot about the posting possibilities for now, and put it to the back of his mind. Whether it was RAF Finningley, RAF Coltishall or RAF St Mawgan, or anywhere else. Clem wasn't bothered. As long as he qualified from RAF Hereford, was all that mattered to him. But there was the added intrigue of the RAF announcing that the Royal Air Force Silver Jubilee celebrations, commemorating Queen Elizabeth II 25 years of royal rule, was to be held at RAF Finningley in July 1977, which was next summer. Clem reckoned that a lot of staff would be required to prepare for that historic occasion, and he put two and two together, and gathered his first choice of RAF Finningley, was a nailed on certainty.

Christmas was coming up quickly, and the supply training course was rapidly gathering speed, to its full conclusion. Clem was to have two weeks off from the course, and he planned to spend it at home, with his family. He had no plans to stay at RAF Hereford, *although it was the Christmas break, the station was still open for the SAS crews to train and manoeuvre,* but Clem was looking forward to getting away from it all, after six weeks at the training camp, as he needed some home comforts again. The supply trade training course for the remaining few days, was purely composed of revising the facts and figures, *and theory*.

To say it was boring, was an understatement, thought Clem. He had got more fun out of watching paint dry. But the revision had to be done and he gritted his teeth and got on with it. At least he had the WRAFs to cheer him up, *even though he had no luck with any of them.*

"The Things We Do For Love" by 10cc and "You're More Than A Number In My Little Red Book," by The Drifters replaced Abba's "Money Money Money" in the race for the most popular song being played. They were both playing everywhere. These songs also helped Clem get through the tedious slog of revision, and he couldn't wait for Christmas. He had no idea what he was getting. He hoped for some aftershave, namely Blue Stratos, and a sheepskin coat. Other than those items, he wasn't too concerned. At seventeen, nearly eighteen years old, he was a bit too long in the tooth for Father Christmas filling his pillow case, with numerous stocking fillers.

When the time came to break off for the Christmas holiday, everyone was relieved, including Corporal McCauley, as his voice was dry and hoarse, and the amount of strain on his vocal chords had taken its toll. He was glad for the Christmas break, even if it was only to re-charge his voice battery. He was also looking forward to pounding the streets of Dublin, where he lived. He had missed pounding the Dublin streets, as he didn't venture home as often as he liked. But he was determined to make up for it, this Christmas.

Clem arrived home on Christmas Eve, and looked forward to two weeks off, until 7th January. The weather was icy, and on Christmas Day, Clem was presented with a lovely long, warm, brown sheepskin coat, with a layer of cream fur inside, and it was snug and cosy, ideal for the freezing cold conditions outside. The Blue Stratos aftershave turned up too, along with soap on a rope, socks, underpants, slippers, Denim and Hai Karate aftershaves, a long sleeved shirt, jeans and a Hotspur comic annual book. It was a good batch of presents for a seventeen year old, thought Clem. And his face was a picture of delight, with gratitude. Christmas was here, in a flash, and gone just as quickly. The celebrations carried on throughout to the New Year, when Clem didn't do anything out of the ordinary, on New Year's Eve. At seventeen, he still wasn't allowed to drink alcohol, and although he had done so in the past, from the age of fifteen, he didn't particularly like drinking, although that of course could all change, as he got older. He remembered the time his brother took him to the Bierkellar, in Hull city centre, when he was aged sixteen, and he drank two large bottles of Newcastle Brown Ale, and was as sick as a dog, and had the hangover from Hell afterwards, and he vowed then, not to touch alcohol again, and he had stuck by his word, ever since.

Before Clem knew it, he was back at RAF Hereford once again, for the second part of the supply trade training course, equipped with his Christmas presents, including the sheepskin coat.

The weather had taken a turn for the worse, and snow was falling, but the rail travel hadn't been affected and Clem made exactly the same journey as he had done seven weeks previously. It took the same amount of time to get there, nearly a full working day, and the same amount of changes, at Stalybridge, Stockport and Crewe. But Clem didn't mind. He enjoyed travelling, and he knew where the platforms were, where the train was, for his connection, and it was as easy as shelling peas. The weather didn't get him down neither, as his sheepskin coat kept him warm and snug.

Once Clem had arrived at RAF Hereford, he headed as usual to the NAAFI shop, where he bought a hot steak pie, a bag of chips, a can of Coca Cola and a carton of milk. He placed the milk in his pocket and ate the pie and chips on the way back to the billet block, after sprinkling salt and vinegar all over the piping hot food. The snow was falling quickly, and large flakes of snow landed on Clem's meal, cooling it down, as he quickly made his way back to the sanctuary of the billet. The heavens had opened, and the snow was beginning to settle and lay everywhere. It was a beautiful sight to see, but treacherous underfoot. Clem thought he had escaped the dangerous conditions of the icy path, but just as he was ready to enter the safety of the billet block, his feet slipped, and he was sent crashing down to the ground, with a terrific thud. He fell awkwardly and landed on the left hand side of his body, with his hip taking the brunt of the fall, and he was cushioned well by his thick sheepskin coat, *and the carton of milk*. But when Clem clambered back up to his feet again, he felt dismayed, as there was a slight wet patch on the outside of his brand new coat, adjacent to the pocket, and when Clem felt with his hand inside, he was horrified to find that the milk had burst open from out of the carton, and filled it half full with the creamy white substance, leaving him feeling sad, gutted and angry, all at once. The area near his coat pocket, was in such a terrible state, and the milk was beginning to leave a nasty dark stain on the outer leather fabric too, making it clearly visible to the eye.

Clem was even more annoyed. Not with himself, but with the weather, the milk and the conditions underfoot. *But it was, what it was, and it was too late now, to cry over the spilled milk.*

He entered the billet, headed for the ablutions and washed out the remaining milk from his coat pocket, with warm soapy water, hoping the nasty stain would disappear. But he wasn't going to hold his breath. He dried the pocket inside and out, the best he could, with paper towels, and waited for it to dry overnight.

Next morning, after Clem's uneasy night in his bunk, where he struggled to get comfortable on the lumpy, bumpy mattress of the single bed, and this coupled with the heat in the billet, which was switched up to high, due to the wintery conditions outside, Clem reckoned he was lucky if he got an hour's sleep. He stepped out of his bed, to check on the condition of his new sheepskin coat, *after the spillage last night*, and he was gutted to discover as expected, that it had left an ugly black mark on the outer skin, which was unsightly, and clearly visible. What with this and his poor night's sleep, he wished he was back in his double bed at home, with all the comforts of an easy family life, until he got a grip of himself, shook the negativity out of his system, and got on to prepare for the working day ahead.

The training got easier, the revision settled down accordingly, and the course whizzed by. It wasn't long before Clem was out in the NAAFI bar, celebrating his 18th birthday. The beer was flowing, the banter was typical of a boozy night, and it was a shame that Clem's birthday fell on a Tuesday, as everyone was going to suffer with an hangover in the morning. Even Clem had indulged in a pint or two of the Stella Artois lager. But it didn't matter, as the training course had finished earlier that same day. *And tonight, it was a double celebration.*

Clem had been, as expected, posted to RAF Finningley, and he remembered the exact time and place where he was, and what he was doing, when he heard of the first posting of his Royal Air Force career. He was balancing nervously back on his chair, leaning on the two hind legs, in a reverse motion, and when Corporal McCauley announced his name and posting, Clem was so shocked, that he flipped backwards on his chair and crashed to the ground, with a thud.

The whole class of trainees erupted into fits of laughter, and Clem struggled to his feet, in complete embarrassment. He wasn't sure why he was so shocked, as he had expected to be posted to RAF Finningley, the second he scribbled it down on to the paper.

The birthday celebrations continued, and nobody gave a jot about the training course. It was over. Everyone had been successful. There were no shocks there. Even "Slap Happy" Jappy made it through successfully.

The party was going great guns. "Flower of Scotland" could be heard loudly in the background, as the Scots were celebrating Burns Night tonight too, in their own inimitable way, and the WRAFs that had been invited to the leaving do, and Clem's birthday bash, got involved in the wild celebrations, downing pints, sinking shorts, and making animals of themselves. They were worse than the blokes. The Stella Artois lager was like nectar to Clem's lips. He wished he had discovered this drink sooner. He managed to finish off three pints, which was better than two, his previous record, and it was a good job and all, as Clem was dunked unceremoniously into an ice cold bath, as part of his 18th birthday celebrations, on his immediate return to the billet block.

Clem was grabbed, by both the arms and legs, by Alf, Peter and Gordon and carried off to the bath, that had been specially prepared earlier, and it was filled with snow and ice from outside. Clem screamed with laughter, as the Stella Artois kicked in, and it assisted in numbing the effects of the freezing cold water, as he was dunked inside the bath, without any mercy shown, whatsoever. It was a fitting end to the training course, and an equally fitting conclusion to Clem's 18th birthday celebrations, as everyone looked forward, ahead, to their postings.

Alf "Joe" King was posted to RAF Wittering.
Gordon "Gin" Bottle was posted to RAF Marham.
Peter "Squeaky" Bird was posted to RAF Brize Norton.
Luke "Slap Happy" Jappy was posted to RAF Scampton.
Clem Harrison was posted to RAF Finningley.
Daniel MacJames was posted to RAF Halton.
Norman Shepherd was posted to RAF Coltishall.
Gerry Joseph was posted to RAF St Mawgan.
Simon Roberts was posted to RAF Leeming.
Noah Williams was posted to RAF Linton on Ouse.
Abraham Wray was posted to RAF Cranwell.
Jack Pott was posted to RAF Coningsby.
Paul Craven was posted to RAF Stafford.
John Carter was posted to RAF Lossiemouth.

The End

Printed in Great Britain
by Amazon